The Ten Commandments of Business Transformation

Practical Advice for Executives Leading Enterprise Change

Patrick Cumby
Rosalind Lambeth

VECTOR PRESS

The Ten Commandments of Business Transformation

© 2012 Patrick Cumby
VECTOR PRESS

patrick.cumby@vectorcsp.com
rosalind.lambeth@vectorcsp.com

Contents

Foreword

Charles Harris

The pace of change in today's world is unprecedented. Consider for a moment how quickly leading organizations have fallen by the wayside. Indeed, as I write this, Sony and Panasonic are forecast to lose more than $15-18 Billion dollars this year while Samsung is forecast to gain similar amounts. In 2012, Kodak – an icon of the photography industry – is closing its doors. Blockbuster Video, a juggernaut of the video rental business is outflanked by Red Box; Red Box is outflanked by NetFlix. Amazon and Google are outflanking everyone!

Clearly, some extraordinarily talented people were caught unaware or (more likely) unable to adapt quickly enough to the swirling currents of change.

Many texts have been written that purport to show leaders the path to organizational change. Many leaders have embarked on such journeys only to find themselves frustrated, adrift and left with an incomplete or less-than-optimal organization – in some cases worse than the original! In the tale contained in this book, the entertaining efforts of King Arthur to manage significant organizational change are more truthful than humorous!

From my personal perspective as the lead executive in a 600+ person organization, making the necessary process changes such that our group could thrive in the future proved both exhilarating and exhausting. What served as my salvation was to articulate clearly and succinctly what our path ahead would require and why we needed to stay focused on that path. In our case, we were faced with an ever-increasingly predatory marketplace where vendors were fighting over a decreasing work share. For the rank-and-file that work share translated directly into job security. Thus, identifying the threat and visualizing a future state where that threat would be negated, served as the launching pad for our organizational re-design project.

However, as they say, the "devil is in the details". Most of us respond in visceral fashion to visions and goals; what frustrates us is our ability (or lack thereof) in translating those visions into executable programs. The Ten Commandments of Business Transformation is that missing connection between the beauty of the ideal and the harsh reality of achieving that ideal. One must never forget that change is inherently unstable; the pressure to return to a more benign status quo is unending (hence the exhaustion mentioned earlier). Each step on the path ahead is marked by guerrilla activity designed to discredit the new order. Thus, having a plan of action and steps along the way is crucial. That plan keeps focus on both the "forest" and the "trees" and does not allow deviations to change our vision.

The desired end state of a transformed organization is not to reach some plateau. Rather the end state is really a <u>state of awareness</u> such that feedback mechanisms ensure continuous improvement. This

Continuous Improvement, done properly with the commensurate performance measures and tools for immediate feedback, is the "new order". Such an end state is the best insulation against those turbulent currents swirling around our organizations. For if we are able to measure those currents, we can adapt quickly; moreover, if we can <u>anticipate</u> those currents, we are even better positioned to thrive in the future.

In the context of the original Ten Commandments, one might say the end state is for everyone to live a peaceful and virtuous life; i.e. to thrive. In the case of the Ten Commandments of Business Transformation, the objective is likewise to reach an end state that ensures our organizations thrive.

These Ten Commandments of Business Transformation will prove vital as you embark on your journey. I am sure you too will enjoy the trip and find the end state exhilarating!

CSH
Stafford, VA
2012

Prologue: Trouble in Camelot!

932 A.D.

The wars are finally over. All of England is now consolidated under one king, and peace flows throughout the land for the first time since... well, ever. The victory feasts and celebrations are winding down and the entire kingdom is looking expectantly to the court at Camelot to usher in a new era of prosperity. King Arthur Pendragon is a wise man, and he realizes that with the end of the wars, he faces a challenge far more complex and subtle than storming castles and laying siege to cities. Now he has to run a country, and convert his wartime armies into peacetime leaders and administrators.

The knights who fought for him, and to whom he owes his success, are men of action. They are warriors, not bureaucrats. Their restlessness threatens to become petty bickering, and a return to the fractured political landscape that Arthur fought so valiantly to eliminate.

King Arthur's problem is this: *the old way of doing things is quickly turning into a liability.* The world has changed, and so must change the attitudes and behaviors of the people running his kingdom -- the knights and the administrative public servants beneath them. To make matters worse, the wars have depleted his treasury, and the new taxation system is spotty at best, meaning that his future budgets are uncertain.

Arthur must take immediate and drastic action. Working within his limited and uncertain budget, and without alienating any of the powerful and restless knights, he must accomplish three goals:

1. Restructure and reorganize for sustainability in the new, unified kingdom.
2. Institute all-new governance structures, policies, processes and procedures in order to dramatically change the behavior of the royal court.
3. Modernize the administrative infrastructure to reflect the new realities. Technology, facilities, tools, equipment all must be upgraded.

His time to enforce these changes is limited; already the momentum of his wartime leadership is starting to fade. The knights and members of the court are beginning to jockey for power in the new organization. Lancelot, Arthur's most loyal lieutenant, is his greatest champion and believes firmly in Arthur's vision for a peaceful kingdom governed by a common law. Percival, on the other hand, has always been a thorn in Arthur's side, and even now he resists Arthur's efforts at establishing a consistent operating model within the organization.

This resistance becomes public one day while the knights are seated at the square council table at Camelot.

"My Lord," Percival argues, "Each of the knights should be free to govern the territories you gave them to their own desires, so long as he pays his due tribute to the king."

Many knights nod at this suggestion, and all look to Lancelot, who shakes his head. "We must all work together for the greater good. Our methods and processes

8

must be aligned in order to ensure the highest service to the kingdom at the lowest cost."

Percival looks around the table. "That's easy for you to say. You have the king's favor and were granted the choicest lands, with educated farmers and ripe fields and orchards. I have to govern a much poorer division, one with a surly workforce and rocky fields, and I must be free to increase productivity as I see fit."

This confrontation set off a series of arguments between Lancelot and Percival that threaten to disrupt the affairs of the court. For now, most of the members of the court prefer to remain bystanders, waiting to see which knight gains the upper hand, noble Lancelot or ambitious Percival. But at every meeting, the knights jostle to sit at the same side of the table as either Lancelot or Percival. Alliances are obviously being formed, and it troubles Arthur greatly that many of the knights are following Percival's lead in treating their baronies as their own mini-kingdoms -- theirs to govern as they see fit.

So far none has seen fit to challenge noble Lancelot, but Arthur can clearly see that the day is coming when this strife will tear his organization apart. His vision of a unified kingdom, the vision for which he fought many battles and shed much blood, is being torn apart.

A Symbol for Change

"I just can't seem to get it into their thick skulls what I'm trying to accomplish," he complains to his wife Guinevere one night while they lie in the royal bedchambers.

"I want them to all be equal, can't they see that? The whole idea was to create a common model under which all my knights operate. But they can't seem to let go of the old ways, and their own individual ambitions are starting to turn them into petty empire-builders."

Guinevere considered this for a long time, in silence. Arthur waited patiently, for he knew she was wise and he trusted her intuition. Finally she spoke. "You need a symbol. A symbol of your vision for the new kingdom."

"What kind of symbol?"

"One that clearly represents justice and equality. One that you can use to rally the knights and the court to your cause."

"Oh, you mean like the royal banner I used in my wartime campaign."

She thought about that. "No, it must be completely different. You are trying for something new, so your symbol must be innovative and fresh, and invoke a passionate emotional response. You say you want justice and equality for all, you want to empower your knights, but you also want them to work together for the greater good. You need a symbol that embodies that vision."

It came to him later that night in a dream. A council of equal knights, all seated at a round table, round so that no knight will have prominence over any of his peers. The decisions of the Council of the Round Table would be binding upon all.

This would be his symbol: King Arthur and the Knights of the Round Table!

Consulting the Expert

Arthur is wise enough to know when to ask for advice, so after lunch the next day he summons his most trusted management consultant, a man who is a real wizard at solving business problems and dealing with prickly organizational behavior issues: Merlin.

Merlin arrives at court in a smart three-piece robe with a black leather briefcase. The courtiers eye him and whisper suspiciously amongst themselves. If Merlin is here, something is up. Arthur only calls in these high-priced consultants when something serious is afoot.

Arthur waves Merlin into his private office and describes his vision of the Round Table over mugs of mead. "I'm not sure how to make it happen. Sure, I can commission my artisans to build me a round table and force the knights to sit at it, but that won't eliminate the problem. I need to capture their hearts and minds, I need to change their operating paradigm, modify their behavior and underlying motivations. That's not so easy to do, especially with this bunch of noble knuckleheads."

Merlin listens carefully before responding. "Change is hard, your Greatness, especially the kind of deep cultural and behavioral change that you so desire. Eight times out of ten the kind of transformation you describe is doomed to failure, for the very reasons you gave, among others. The stark truth is that *large-scale business transformation is the most difficult task you will ever face as a leader.*"

Arthur pounds his fist on his desk, almost spilling his flagon of mead. "I cannot afford to fail. The lives of my subjects depend upon me making this change, taking this organization in a new direction."

Merlin nods solemnly, but then the ends of his mouth curl up in an assured grin. "Do not despair, my Liege, I may have just what you need to succeed."

Arthur looks up at him hopefully. Merlin had pulled successes out of his wizard's hat before.

Prologue: Trouble in Camelot!

"Truly? What spell or incantation can you perform to influence my knights to change?"

"Unfortunately there is no magic charm to ensure the success of an organizational change management initiative. However, there is... this!"

With great ceremony Merlin opens his briefcase and extracts a heavy stone tablet inscribed with a set of strange runes. He carefully places the weighty tablet on Arthur's desk. Arthur eyes it suspiciously. The last mysterious item Merlin had given him had been an April Fool's gift of a flagon of fine wine. Upon opening, it had turned into a chicken and frightened his hunting dogs. Merlin was a well-known prankster.

"What's that?" said Arthur.

"Wisdom, my Lord."

"What kind of wisdom?"

"The kind that will get you out of your current scrape, your Highness. It's the Ten Commandments of Business Transformation."

"Where'd you get it?"

Merlin winks. "Trade secret, Your Royal Highness. Let's just say that it contains the ancient wisdom of the great business sages and change-management gurus like Kotter, Cohen, Kay, Bennis, and others."

"Okay, okay. What does it say?"

Merlin lowers his voice to a hushed tone and reads the tablet. Arthur listens carefully. After Merlin is finished, Arthur looks at him skeptically. "I don't understand these Commandments. How will I apply them to my dilemma?"

Merlin leans back in his chair and winks at the king. "Your Majesty, that's what you have me for. Let me walk you through them, one at a time, starting with Commandment One."

I: Thou shalt develop clear and compelling transformation cornerstones.

Merlin shifts his chair and pulls it closer to Arthur's desk. His jovial tone vanishes and he locks eyes with the king. "Here's the deal, Arthur. The only way that this change is going to happen is for the leaders in your organization to commit the large amount of life energy it takes to make real change. That commitment requires passion in your leaders and acceptance within the workforce.

"The only way you're going to generate that passion is to create a compelling shared vision that clearly and unambiguously states the urgent benefits of success and the dire consequences of failure. Every single person in your kingdom, whether they completely understand it or not, needs to have this vision, and be able to articulate it in ten seconds or less."

Transformation Cornerstones

Merlin continued. "You need to build a foundation for your new business model. And every foundation begins with a set of cornerstones. In a castle, the placement, size, and shape of the cornerstones dictate to the builder the shape and form of the finished building. Just as with the castle architect, so do you need to craft the cornerstones for the form and function of your new kingdom.

"Your Transformation Cornerstones must be simple, clear, and unambiguous, and support your vision for the future. A twelve-year-old squire must be able to recite them in ten seconds. Just like your rallying cry on

I: Thou shalt develop clear and compelling transformation cornerstones.

the battlefield, so are these cornerstones the rallying cry of your transformation effort."

"I know well what my cornerstones are, though I have never thought of them as such."

"Well, then, here's the question of the day: what are your Transformation Cornerstones?"

Arthur thought for a few moments, and then began hesitantly, "Well, I guess I want to restructure and reorganize the Knights into a flat, matrixed organization, and institute new universal policies and procedures, and I'd also like to update the administrative tools..."

"Hold it right there, Sire. These things of which you speak are not transformation cornerstones. They are instead activities that will probably be necessary to implement change. Remember, your Cornerstones should reflect your vision; they should inspire passion in your leadership and workforce. Nobody gets passionate about a reorganization or writing a policy manual. You certainly can't expect a squire or a peasant to understand these things, much less recite them in ten seconds or less."

Arthur admitted grudgingly that Merlin was correct, and asked for an example of a well-defined Cornerstone.

"Let me ask you a question first..."

Arthur interrupted him. "Why do you always answer my questions with another question?"

"Because I'm a consultant, Your Highness. Now, tell me, what are you most passionate about? What really gets your blood boiling with excitement?"

"God, Crown, and Country, of course. Defense of the realm. Justice and fairness. Fighting evil. Chivalry."

Merlin leans back with a wide grin. "Bingo, Sire, you've hit the nail on the head. Those concepts must be

I: Thou shalt develop clear and compelling transformation cornerstones.

the basis of your cornerstones, because they describe the new kingdom you want to create using familiar terms that everyone can understand."

He handed Arthur a slate and a soapstone marker. "Write down the cornerstone principles that are necessary to realize your vision so that the rest of the kingdom can behold them. But be sparing with your words; if you have more than four or five cornerstones you dilute their importance."

Arthur scratched the following onto a slate:
1. Peerage among the knights
2. Equal justice for all subjects
3. The Code of Chivalry
4. Defense of Crown and Country

Merlin read the list and nodded. "Good. We can work with this. Now, keep in mind that these are the ideals, they represent the grand vision. Having a vision is a good thing, but you must be able to turn vision into reality, and this takes action from your leadership and workforce. You must guide these actions carefully to ensure that every task, every expenditure of resources is aligned with one or more of your Cornerstones. Every decision you or your leaders make, every resource you expend, should be judged by its alignment with the Cornerstones. In short, you must give your leaders enough information so that they can judge whether or not their actions are aligned with the Cornerstones."

"And how do I do that?"

Cornerstone Objectives

Merlin's eyes twinkled – he obviously relished the role of guru to the king. "Well, sire, you've got to break down each cornerstone into a set of transformational

---

I: Thou shalt develop clear and compelling transformation cornerstones.

Cornerstone Objectives. Think of the objectives as the individual building blocks of the Cornerstone. They become the measure of your success. That's how you'll know if you have attained a Cornerstone, when all of the Cornerstone Objectives have been completed."

Some of these words sounded familiar to Arthur. "It sounds like you're talking about creating a wartime strategy. Goals and objectives and such."

Merlin nodded. "Yes, exactly. But instead of creating a strategy for how you will conquer the enemy, you're creating a strategy specifically for how you will transform your organization and your workforce."

Arthur's eyes lit up. "So, just like in battle, we'll need a plan of attack, a battlefield map, success criteria..."

Merlin interrupted him with a chuckle. "Yes, you're getting the idea. But you are getting ahead of yourself. Before you start drawing your roadmap or plan of attack, you've got to take the time to get the fundamentals right."

Arthur nodded impatiently; he wasn't used to being chided by one of his subjects, but he was wise enough to know when to shut up and listen. "Sorry to interrupt. Keep going."

The 'So What?' Test

"So, where were we? Ah yes, Cornerstone Objectives. Each objective should be phrased so that it is clear, unambiguous, and have clearly defined success criteria. Most importantly, so that you can counter the arguments of Percival and his foot-dragging ilk, each objective must be able to pass the 'So What?' test."

"What's that?"

I: Thou shalt develop clear and compelling transformation cornerstones.

"For each objective you must ask yourself, 'So What?' What value does the objective have? What is the compelling and urgent benefit of achieving the objective? If it doesn't pass the 'So What?' test, you'll never be able to convince Percy's people to make it a priority."

Arthur looks at Merlin with a furrowed brow and a frown. "I don't get it. Give me an example."

"Sure thing. Let's take your first Cornerstone, 'Peerage Among the Knights.' How do you plan to achieve this Cornerstone?"

Arthur thought about this. "Well, I have this idea for a round table at Camelot for the knights to use when in council."

"Ah, yes, the round table idea. Tell me, Arthur, what problem does the round table solve?

Arthur raises an eyebrow. "Can you not see the answer yourself?"

"Yes, I think I know the reason, but I need to hear it from you. As king, your objectives must not be open to interpretation. If you leave wiggle room, people might misunderstand your intent. Worse yet, Sir Percy or someone like him will use the ambiguity to subvert your desires."

"There is no head to a round table. One seat is equal to all other seats. The round table symbolizes equality for all the knights."

Merlin produces a blank scroll out of his briefcase and scratches notes with a quill pen. He writes:

Cornerstone: Peerage Among the Knights

Cornerstone Objective 1: Install a round table at Camelot for the Knights Council to represent the Kingdom's core values of equality, unity, comradeship and singleness of purpose of all the Knights.

I: Thou shalt develop clear and compelling transformation cornerstones.

Arthur looks at the words Merlin has written. "That's a lot of words."

"Yes, unlike the cornerstones, you need to make sure the Transformation Objectives have enough substance to be unambiguous." Merlin went on to describe how every objective should be carefully worded so as to convey what you're trying to accomplish, how you are going to accomplish it, and the compelling and urgent reason for the accomplishment.

"The other thing to remember is that objectives must be concrete and achievable, and it should be obvious when they are accomplished so your constituents can recognize success. That's why you must never have a fluffy objective like 'All knights must demonstrate unity and equality.' Vague objectives like that are simply too difficult to measure."

"This is hard," complains Arthur.

"Yes it is very hard, but this is far and away the most important thing you will ever do as king, so don't take it lightly. Spend the time and effort to get it right. If you don't, then you and your kingdom will suffer great consequences as your leaders start spending resources without fully understanding your vision, and more importantly, the purpose that drives it."

Arthur nods. "This I well know. My knights are all men of action; they constantly start new projects without sufficient planning. Even now they are all going in conflicting directions. Dear Lancelot, in his zeal to make me happy, has gone down a path that is not completely aligned with my wishes, and is wasting precious resources."

"Alignment and efficient use of resources during times of change is critical. As a military leader, you understand how important it is for your army to all march in the same direction and executing the same strategy." Merlin points to the stone tablet. "This brings us to Commandment Two."

II: Thou shalt understand the best-practice methods for managing change.

Merlin steeples the fingers of both hands in a classic lecturer's pose and looks over them at Arthur. "As you so rightly declare, my king, one of the biggest challenges you face is keeping your eager knights from going off willy-nilly in a hundred different directions in their efforts to please you."

"Or thwart me, as seems to be the case with Percival," mutters Arthur.

"Even so, but pure Lancelot may also unknowingly thwart you by simply misunderstanding the change-management methodology. It will be difficult, but you must limit change-related activity until you have defined your business transformation roadmap."

"But we cannot wait to start. Time is passing quickly and the clarity of my vision is waning within the knights. I must act now!

"My Liege, do you fire the catapult at the enemy castle wall without first ensuring it is in range? Without aiming it? Without loading it with a missile?"

"Of course not!" Arthur fumes at Merlin's brazen impertinence. He briefly imagines the wizard hanging from shackles on the ramparts of Camelot. But then he dismisses the mental image; he needs Merlin, and will put up with the consultant's insolence—for now.

Merlin ignores Arthur's scowl and continues. "Allowing your knights to begin business transformation activities without following a proven methodology will have much the same result as firing an unloaded arbalest: embarrassment and potential defeat. Imagine what silly

---

II: Thou shalt understand the best-practice methods for managing change.

things Lancelot will do, or what Percy and his cronies will get away with, if you don't have an underlying methodology to manage the change effort and enforce accountability for change?

"So how do I keep my knights from proceeding down the wrong path while they wait for a plan?"

"The answer is simple. Don't make them wait. Involve them in the planning process. Let them know that they are all key participants a planning phase of an over-arching change management process. This will have several advantages. First, it makes them aware of the methodology and gives them a sense of ownership of the process. Plus, this won't be the last change your kingdom will endure, and having a leadership cadre that is aware of change management best practices will greatly improve the quality of overall leadership."

"You keep mentioning a methodology. Is this wizard-speak for some consulting service you are trying to sell me?"

Merlin ignores the royal insinuation. "As in war, Your Highness, you can't have a winning business transformation plan without first defining a strategy and an approach. On the battlefield you have a vision of victory, you have a strategy to take the castle, and you have a methodology, or a process, to execute the strategy.

"Change management is no different. Now that you have defined your Transformation Cornerstones and Objectives, you have the overall strategy for your change. Next you need to select the proven, best-practice methodology you will use to actually implement the change."

Once again, Merlin leans close and lowers his voice. "Now pay attention, your Eminence. The method of

which I speak is not the same thing as the change
management plan itself. Instead, it is the fundamental
process that guides the creation and execution of the plan.
It is the proven, best-practice approach that you employ
to manage the change project.

Change Management IS Project Management

"In fact, you must think of *change management* as
a flavor of *project management*. Like any other project, a
change management project has a beginning, middle, and
end, produces an outcome, and comprises activities that
require resources to complete. Just like building a castle,
there are performance, schedule, and cost constraints,
and there are issues and risks to be mitigated. You will
also need a blueprint to work from, and a way to measure
progress toward milestones.

"When you built Camelot, I'd be willing to bet that
the project management methodology could have been
broken down into the four phases." Merlin scratches more
words onto the slate:

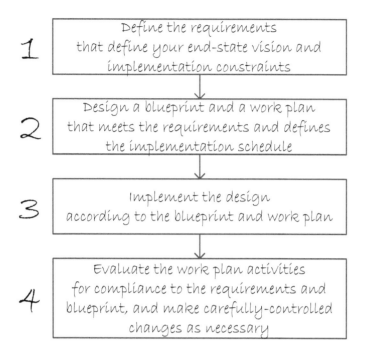

1 — Define the requirements that define your end-state vision and implementation constraints

2 — Design a blueprint and a work plan that meets the requirements and defines the implementation schedule

3 — Implement the design according to the blueprint and work plan

4 — Evaluate the work plan activities for compliance to the requirements and blueprint, and make carefully-controlled changes as necessary

Arthur examines the scribbles and nods. "You speak the truth."

Merlin continued. "The change management process is exactly the same, except that instead of building a castle, you are building a new culture by changing the behavior of your leaders and the workforce. There are many change management theories, approaches, and methodologies, and they all require the application of sound project management practices to be successful.

II: Thou shalt understand the best-practice methods for managing change.

Change Management Phases and Outputs

"Let's walk through the four project management phases and discuss the outputs from a business transformation perspective."

1. Requirements Definition

"First, you must define the high-level transformational requirements for the end-state organization."

"The Cornerstones from Commandment One," observes Arthur.

Merlin raises an eyebrow. "Very good, your Majesty! You're correct! The Cornerstones and Cornerstone Objectives represent your high-level transformational requirements, and will guide the development of the blueprint and work plan."

Arthur knits his kingly brow. "What do you mean by blueprint? I thought a blueprint was a drawing that describes a building."

2. Business Architecture Modeling

Merlin nods. "In business transformation, a blueprint describes the desired end-state of the business operational model in much the same way as a construction blueprint shows the structural details of a castle. I call it the Operations Blueprint, and it defines your organization chart and process model. It shows the details about how all of the components of your kingdom should be performing and how they will interact with each other. It is, in effect, the basis of your 'to-be' enterprise architecture. We'll talk more about the blueprint in Commandment Five.

II: Thou shalt understand the best-practice methods for managing change.

3. Transformation Planning

"Once you have an Operations Blueprint, you are ready to develop the transformation plan. The plan must include a detailed breakdown of the activities and resources required to operationalize the blueprint. Components of the plan will include a high-level Roadmap you can use to educate your stakeholders, and a detailed Master Schedule that you'll use to manage resources and track progress. We'll discuss these in more detail in Commandments Seven and Eight.

4. Implementation and Evaluation

"When the Blueprint, Roadmap, and Master Schedule are complete you are then, and only then, fully prepared to start transforming the organization. Commandments Nine and Ten discuss the use of information management systems and dashboards to enforce accountability for change and measure progress toward achieving each Cornerstone Objective."

"Merlin, I am beginning to suspect that you are making all this up to gain my favor."

"Not at all, your Majesty. While my methods may be more practical than most, there are many wizards in the world who have developed excellent approaches to change management. It is a good idea for you as king to do a little research and have at least a passing familiarity with them. Look for books by John Kotter, Dan Cohen, Warren Bennis, Chris Argyris, and others.

Arthur shook his head. "I will read these books as time permits. But I am no expert on these change management methods, and neither are my knights. Nor do any of us have the time or the inclination to spend reading multiple tomes to become an expert."

II: Thou shalt understand the best-practice methods for managing change.

Merlin nods agreement. "This brings us to Commandment Three," he says, "My personal favorite of the ten."

III: Thou shalt empower dedicated transformation management resources.

erlin points at the thick stone walls of the king's office. "What means were required to build your great castle, my Lord?"

The king's face lights up; Arthur is rightly proud of his castle. "I summoned the greatest builders and artisans in all Briton to create my citadel. I commissioned a great quarry at Glastonbury to harvest the stones. I employed the finest weavers to create my tapestries..."

Merlin interrupts the king. "In other words, you brought in external resources because your organic workforce had neither the skill nor the extra bandwidth to accomplish the task."

Arthur nods proudly. "Yes, in order to build the greatest castle in the world I hired the greatest engineers in all Christendom."

Merlin smiles, for he has Arthur right where he wants him. "Your Greatness, building the culture you desire at Camelot will be just as difficult as building the ramparts of Camelot. It will require specialized methods and expertise and the expenditure of extra labor hours over and above your normal workload. Where you needed master builders, carpenters, stonemasons, and laborers for the Camelot construction project, for a business transformation project you need a strong project manager, analysts, instructional designers, instructors, not to mention a significant investment of time and energy from your current workforce."

III: Thou shalt empower dedicated transformation management resources.

Dedicated Transformation Management Resources

Arthur scowls. "My knights and their lieutenants should be capable of implementing my vision. They are heroic and accomplished men of valor."

"Could your knights have built the castle of Camelot?"

"Of course not! They are not common laborers! They are fully tasked by their royal duties and responsibilities. They neither have the time nor the temperament to raise a castle..." Arthur's voice trails off as he watches Merlin's grin grow wider. "But this is your point, isn't it."

Merlin nods with satisfaction. "Precisely, my Liege! Business Transformation is a discipline that requires specialized skills, knowledge, and tools."

Merlin scratches a diagram on the king's slate.

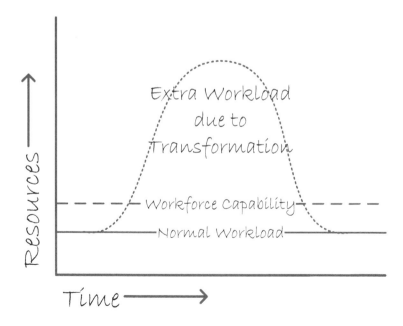

III: Thou shalt empower dedicated transformation management resources.

"Look here, your Grace. Enterprise-wide transformation demands of your workforce a large commitment of time and energy over-and-above what is required for their normal duties, especially from your leadership and management – extra time and energy that impacts their ability to complete their traditional daily workload. Burdening them with such a complex task for which they possess neither the ability nor time is setting them up for failure."

Merlin's voice assumes the serious tone he uses when he wants to make an important point. "Your Royalness, most large-scale business transformation efforts fail miserably. The reason? Because they are not properly resourced to handle the extra workload of transformation. To be successful, you need two things: an expert change manager with authority of the king, and a set of chartered and resourced implementation teams within your workforce to perform the extra workload required during the duration of the transformation project. In simple terms, you need a specialist to MANAGE the change project, and you need a team of trusted change agents within the workforce to IMPLEMENT the change-related activities."

Dedicated Change-Manager

The king starts to speak but Merlin is in lecture mode and dismisses him with a wave of his hand. "First, you need an accomplished and impartial project manager who is familiar with the change management discipline. This individual must lead you and your knights through the methodology we discussed in Commandment Two. It is this person's job to manage the process of change so that it can occur without major impact to your

---

III: Thou shalt empower dedicated transformation management resources.

organization's productivity or service to its customers. After all, you cannot stop defending your realm or producing food for your subjects while you reorganize your workforce."

Arthur chuckles. "True enough. A well-fed peasant labors hard and thinks nothing of revolt."

Merlin nods agreement. "The Transformation Manager role is very important. It must be dedicated; it cannot be a collateral duty or an afterthought. Empowering a dedicated manager sends a message to your stakeholders that you are serious about the change initiative. It is also critical to have someone whose *only* job is to pay attention to the complex tasks, risks, and issues that characterize a business transformation project. You wouldn't build a castle without a construction foremen, so don't try to implement a complex organizational and cultural change without someone managing the process."

Arthur furrowed his brow. "So this so-called Transformation Manager would do what? Guide and educate my leadership and management on the mysteries of change management?"

"Guide and educate, yes, but also cajole, embarrass, threaten – whatever it takes to achieve the Transformation Cornerstone Objectives," says Merlin. "Just like your castle construction foreman, your Transformation Manager must be empowered by you to enforce your will and act with your authority when it comes to holding your leaders accountable to the Cornerstone Objectives. Without your unambiguous public support, no one at court will heed him, especially not your strong-willed knights."

III: Thou shalt empower dedicated transformation management resources.

Arthur narrowed his eyes in suspicion. "And I suppose you would be just the man for the job."

Merlin coughed delicately. "Well, my Liege, since you bring it up, I would be honored to play this critical role."

"Thought so," muttered Arthur.

"But I would not take the job unless you commit to giving me the resources I need for success. Depending on the scope and scale, it may require a small team of analysts to define the new business model, policies, processes and metrics for your Operations Blueprint. I will also likely need to employ instructional designers to develop training, instructors to deliver training, and writers to create process and procedure guides."

Arthur sighed. "And I thought installing a round table would be a simple matter."

"But wait, Your Greatness, even a dedicated transformation management team is not enough. To maximize your chances of success you must also allocate resources to implement the change activities within the bowels of your organization. The kind of sweeping change you envisage will require coordinated teamwork from change agents scattered throughout your enterprise. The change manager can only manage the process—your organization must do the work to implement the changes."

The Change Implementation Teams

"To be most effective, change must come from within. If the workforce contributes to the change process instead of having it imposed from above, then they feel a sense of ownership.

III: Thou shalt empower dedicated transformation management resources.

"For this reason, Sire, you need to charter Change Implementation Teams within key areas of your organization. Each of these teams must be led by a change agent, someone who understands both your vision for the change and the intricacies of his or her own area of the organization.

"You must make your expectations clear to these change agents: *they must implement the transformation roadmap without interrupting service to their customers.* Remember, most business transformation projects fail because the workforce perceives the required activities as a collateral duty, secondary to their regular 'day job.' You should not expect your subjects to completely disregard their traditional daily activities to engage in transformation, but the hard truth is that during the transformation project, they must accomplish both. This will require extra commitment from them.

"How much extra commitment should I expect from them?" asked Arthur. "Are we talking overtime here?"

"Well, they may be required to spend several hours in each workday attending meetings, participating in training exercises, or working other tasks related to the transformation. In many cases, they must make up this time by working longer hours each day."

"They aren't going to like that," growled Arthur.

"Of course not. To keep them motivated, you must continually reward and recognize them throughout the duration for their extra service. It is up to your Change Implementation Teams, working with the Transformation Manager, to figure out how to achieve this delicate balance; how they will do what it takes to make the change without jeopardizing service to the customer."

III: Thou shalt empower dedicated transformation management resources.

Arthur looked glum. "Many of my knights barely talk to each other. How can I expect them to all work together?"

Merlin shook his head in sympathy. "Maintaining alignment among your stakeholders is a serious challenge. One of the most critical tasks for your Transformation Manager and his implementation teams is communicating priorities and urgency to leadership, the workforce, and all their constituents. Which brings us to Commandment Four."

III: Thou shalt empower dedicated transformation management resources.

IV: Thou shalt communicate relentlessly.

The king's expression is gloomy. "Merlin, even those who love me and my vision will find it hard to make the changes I ask of them. People seem to like the idea of change, but few actually enjoy the reality of having their beloved routines and traditions disrupted."

In response to the king's disheartened tone, the sorcerer suddenly leaps from his chair and throws his arms wide over his head. His eyes flash and his voice booms like thunder. "Then you must SCARE them!"

Arthur jerks back in his seat and glares at Merlin as if he were a poisonous snake. "How dare you frighten me like that? You forget your place, wizard!"

Merlin bows apologetically and lowers his voice. "Your pardon, my king, I was only making a point. You can't get people to listen if you don't have their attention. You must convince your workforce by espousing the shining benefits of making the change, and threatening the dire consequences of NOT making the change. A strong, multi-faceted communications plan that pounds the message home over and over and over again is critical to change the behavior of a workforce."

A Sense of Urgency

"It all boils down to this: *there must be a visceral sense of urgency*, strong enough to force even the most cynical employee to make hard, difficult changes to their ingrained behaviors, rituals, and routines. You must make them see that it is impossible for them to continue

IV: Thou shalt communicate relentlessly.

to do business the old way. You must convince them through continuous and consistent words and actions that there is far more pain in continuing along the old path than in adopting the new ways."

"Yes, yes, I understand. I will explain to the court that we risk a return to the old days of warlords and anarchy. "

Merlin shook his head. "That's not good enough, your Highness. In order to instill and maintain a sense of urgency, the perceived consequences of resistance must be immediate and dreadful, and/or the perceived reward for progress must be shining. Remember, you are asking your subjects to abandon many of the behaviors they hold dear for a future state that is unclear to them. Think of stubborn and wily Percival; what stick or carrot is strong enough to sway him, or at least turn his peers against him? What is his greatest fear, and his most desired fantasy?"

"If you ask me, his greatest fear is that his poor farmers will revolt and overthrow him. His greatest desire is, um, probably replacing me as king."

"Then perhaps you should play up the threat of mass starvation, of a peasant revolt. You must carefully construct a message that plays to their greatest fears and shows them the path to their greatest desires. Only then can you inspire the passion necessary to change their culture and world view."

"It's important that you don't just talk about it: SHOW people the way forward. Foretell a short-term future state, and then accomplish it. Then do it again. Demonstrate and celebrate a steady stream of small successes that reinforce the benefits of the new business model, and also broadcast the negative events that occur

IV: Thou shalt communicate relentlessly.

due to the old model, even if you have to carefully engineer the situation to make these positive and negative examples come to pass.

　　Arthur doesn't seem convinced. "But Percy is just one of many people I must convince to support my vision for the kingdom. Getting him to change is important, but he is only one knight. How will the other knights feel about the changes I propose? No doubt some will love my vision and our Transformation Cornerstones, and some will hate them. What about the members of the royal court, and the castle stewards, not to mention the clergy, merchants and peasants? How do I convince them all that it is in their best interest to change their behaviors?"

　　Merlin taps his long fingernails on the edge of the king's desk. "Excellent point, Your Greatness." He picked up the slate and a drew a strange shape with the soapstone marker.

Focus on the Stakeholders who have both Interest and Influence

　　"Do you know what a bell curve is, your Majesty?"

　　Arthur growls. "Of course I do. Don't insult my intelligence. You don't get to be Supreme Ruler and Defender of the Faith without knowing a few things."

　　Merlin lowers his head in respect. "Just so, Your Grace. Think of this bell curve as representing all the stakeholders within your kingdom. Each of them falls into one of three categories: champions, resistors, and bystanders."

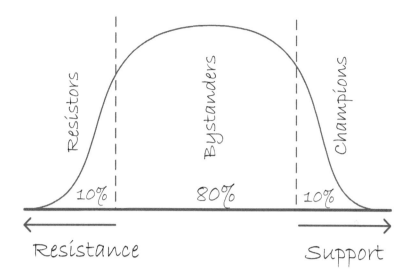

"You will have the support of a few champions, perhaps ten to twenty percent, and you will face the resistance of many outspoken resistors, perhaps another ten to twenty percent. The vast majority at the center of the bell curve, perhaps 80% of the stakeholders, will stand on the sidelines waiting to see who will gain the upper hand. The goal of your marketing and communications plan is simple:

1) Strengthen and empower the champions,
2) Marginalize or silence the resistors, and
3) Sway the bystanders."

Arthur chuckles. "Marginalize or silence, eh? In the old days it would have been simple to silence Percy. A quick thrust of Excalibur would have done the trick quite nicely. But in my new order, I must use words and political maneuvering instead of steel to silence my enemies. To do otherwise would set a terrible example."

Strengthen Champions, Marginalize Resistors

"Very wise, Your Highness. Brain will overcome brawn every time. You need a clever plan to marginalize those that speak out against you and strengthen those that support you, without resorting to messy executions. In order to create such a plan, you will need to take a census of all your stakeholders and constituent groups. Who are they, and what role do they play? Most importantly, you must understand how much power and influence they wield to either support or resist you, and their level of interest in the changes you desire." Merlin wiped away the bell curve drawing with the hem of his robe and again scratched at the slate with the soapstone.

"As you can see, Sire, you can plot your stakeholder interest and power on a graph. Once you know who falls in which quadrant, you can prioritize your change management and communications efforts."

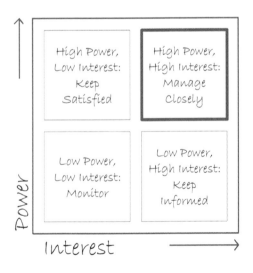

IV: Thou shalt communicate relentlessly.

Arthur studied the graph and pointed to the upper right quadrant. "These are the high-priority individuals, the key players. This is where Percy and Lancelot will fall."

"Exactly! The bishop, the merchant's guild, Percival, Mordred, and Lancelot, among others. You will need to manage these stakeholders carefully. Percival and his followers are powerful and influential resistors; they do not like your vision for the kingdom because it will limit their power to impose their will with impunity within their baronies. The archbishop and the merchants are bystanders; they will remain neutral as long as you do not appear to usurp the power of the Church or the Guild. Lancelot is the largest landholder and your greatest champion.

"It is on these stakeholders that you must concentrate your limited resources. Don't worry too much about the others, such as the lesser knights or the members of your court or the peasants. While it is important to keep them informed, rest assured they will be watching the high-priority stakeholders and will follow whoever seems to be winning the war of words."

Arthur studied the graph and nodded. "Yes, this makes it clear that I need to strengthen Lancelot, consult with the bishop and the merchants, and marginalize Percival and his cronies."

Merlin smiled. "Voila, my king, you now have a change management communications strategy."

Communicate Roles, Accountabilities, and Expectations

"The next step of communications planning requires more attention to detail. Part of your plan must ensure that all stakeholders and all affected members of your workforce have a broad and common understanding of the Transformation Cornerstones and Objectives."

"I will travel the length and breadth of the land and speak in every town and village, if that's what it takes."

"Perfect! Once you have established awareness, all stakeholders must be informed of their individual roles and what part they are expected to play in the transformation process. This may require a detailed version of the stakeholder analysis, a job task analysis, a change impact analysis, or all of the above. Your Transformation Manager and Implementation Teams can help develop this part of the plan.

"Your primary communications objectives are to make your expectations known and to create a sense of accountability in each of the key stakeholders. If they know that you and their supervisors are holding them personally accountable for making the change in their behavior, then their motivation will be stronger."

"Finally, you must provide training or re-training to individuals and groups within the workforce. You cannot expect them to adopt new processes and procedures if they do not understand them or their purpose."

The king thinks about this for a few moments. "You're right, wizard. We'll have to figure out new policies, and how they impact existing job roles and processes. We can't retrain the workforce without knowing how the changes affect their individual jobs."

"You must have read my mind, my Liege," says Merlin, pointing to the stone tablet. "For that is the subject of Commandment Five!"

IV: Thou shalt communicate relentlessly.

V: Thou shalt design
with the end in sight.

erlin leans across the desk toward Arthur. "Commandment Five is a tough one to swallow, your Highness, because compliance will be very costly, both in money and political capital. But, like all the other commandments, it is absolutely crucial to success."

"It wouldn't be the first time your advice gave me indigestion."

Merlin chuckles, and then turns serious. "The single most daunting aspect of managing kingdom-wide transformation is the fact that the changes can impact dozens, even hundreds of jobs, and require retraining the workforce. Not to mention investment in new technology, equipment, facilities, and other infrastructure."

The wizard stands up and folds his arms behind his back; he obviously likes to pace while he lectures.

The Operations Blueprint

"To be successful, your Eminence, you must retrain the workforce, and give them the tools and resources they need to do their jobs the new way. In order to understand how the Transformation Cornerstones and Objectives impact each and every job, you must commission a very detailed job task impact analysis, and then develop discrete job-level procedures for each impacted job. Using this information, you can create the Operations Blueprint that describes the new organizational roles and operational process model.

"Make no mistake; *this is the single most technically challenging and resource-intensive part of business transformation.*"

Merlin stopped pacing and pointed his finger at the king. "If you cannot tell a worker exactly how to do his job, and give him the proper tools, he will not be able to complete the task to your satisfaction, no matter how hard he tries."

Arthur glared at the wizard's pointing finger and the long, manicured fingernail. It was a clear breach of royal etiquette. Merlin realized what he was doing and quickly withdrew his hand. "Sorry, your Majesty. I sometimes get carried away trying to make a point."

Arthur grunted. "Continue."

New Capabilities are Required to Enable New Operational Outcomes

Merlin is silent for a moment, as if considering how best to proceed. He sits down in the chair and leans back. "Let's talk theory for a minute."

"Let's not."

"Humor me, Arthur."

The king sighs. "Fine."

"At its heart, what is the goal of business transformation?"

"Is this a trick question?"

"Of course not."

Arthur thinks. "Implementing a new way of doing business."

Merlin shakes his head. "Of course you are correct your Grace, but let me state it another way. The goal of transformation is to *build the capabilities that enable accomplishment of key operational outcomes.*"

V: Thou shalt design with the end in sight.

48

Arthur considers this for a moment and nods.
"Okay, so what?"

"Think about what I just said. There are two major
ideas in that sentence. The first is the concept of a *key
operational outcome*. The second concept is one of
capability building. In order to build a capability that
enables accomplishment of a key operational outcome,
you must first define the outcome, and then you must
determine the tasks and resources required to build the
capability.

"I call it 'Designing with the End in Sight.' It is a
multi-step process. First your Transformation Manager
works with the Implementation Teams and subject
matter experts in the workforce to document your 'to-be'
business lifecycle. For each phase of the lifecycle they
identify the key operational outcomes required to support
your Cornerstones. Working from this lifecycle map, they
can then begin the arduous task of developing a detailed
process and organizational architecture that enables each
of the outcomes.

"When complete, this business architecture clearly
describes your 'to-be' business model in detailed and
unambiguous terms. It becomes the Operations Blueprint
for your new business model."

Identify the Key Operational Outcomes

Arthur begins to regret summoning the sorcerer,
but knows he has no choice but to endure the lecture.
"But a business model is complex," he argues. "There may
be hundreds of interconnected processes and procedures.
Merchants, clergy, knights, peasants all interact. Amidst
all this complexity, how am I supposed to figure out what
these 'outcomes' are?

V: Thou shalt design with the end in sight.

"There are fewer than you think. Remember, we are talking about *key* outcomes, not *all* outcomes. Think of key outcomes as the ones that enable or force the accomplishment of your Cornerstones. It is on these few transformation drivers that you want to focus your change management resources. If you have more than a dozen for each Cornerstone, you probably have too many.

Define Accountability across Organizational Boundaries

"Once you know the key outcomes of your new business model, you must ask a very important question about each one. Who is responsible for producing the outcome, and what interactions are required between business units and across organizational boundaries to produce the outcome?

"You are talking about accountability, aren't you?" said the king.

"Of course, Sire. Assigning accountability for each outcome is crucial. Someone's reputation and livelihood must be at stake in order for them to feel motivated enough to consistently produce the outcome. But even with clearly assigned ownership, and a motivated employee, the system can fail. Production of an outcome can depend on an input from another business unit over which the accountable person has no control. Unless the person who is responsible for delivering the critical input shares liability with the outcome owner, you cannot enforce accountability.

Merlin notices the king nod slightly, not in understanding, but in stupor. The warmth of the fire and his after-lunch digestive functions are rendering the king sleepy. Merlin raises his voice. "Look, Sire, I know this is

V: Thou shalt design with the end in sight.

getting in the weeds, but it is important for you to understand it so you can back up your Transformation Manager when he encounters resistance. Identifying these organizational boundaries and the cross-boundary dependencies is crucial when assigning accountability, and can be the deciding factor between success and failure of an operations model. And in many cases, *only you as king have the power to force the different business units to cooperate.*

"Addressing this issue in the design phase of a transformation prevents months and years of frustrating and expensive excuses and finger pointing and sets expectations for shared accountability and high organizational performance."

Arthur blinks and refocuses on the magician. "Okay, I get it. It's my job to impose accountability across organizational boundaries. What's next?"

Create Detailed Process and Job Task Definitions

The wizard paces faster. "Now comes the hard part. I call it 'dragging the workforce through the mud.' It's difficult, expensive, and time consuming, but it is without a doubt the best and quickest method to get understanding and buy-in from your employees and stakeholders."

Merlin abruptly stops pacing and spins to face the king. He sprouts an evil grin that is clearly visible beneath his neatly-trimmed goatee. "Here's what to do. Put your Implementation Teams in a locked room with all the subject matter experts and outcome owners, and the cross-boundary stakeholders. Tell them they can't leave the workshop without hashing out a detailed process and procedure model for how they will produce the outcome in the most reliable, cost-effective manner possible. Then sit back and watch the head-banging begin."

"You sound like you enjoy this."

"Most certainly, your Grace. It can be very entertaining watching the stakeholders interact. In my experience, there are usually several individuals in the room who have never met each other before, despite the fact that they each own a crucial step in the overall process. It can sometimes be tough, but with proper facilitation they storm, form, and norm, and soon begin to realize that it's in their best interest to cooperate.

"It's like watching a candle being lit. At first there's a lot of sputtering, but by the end, there is consensus, everyone has a deep understanding of the outcome and its processes and job tasks, and all the parties feel an emotional ownership for the model that they labored to create. Plus, having spent time together in a tough environment, they begin to gel as a team. Yes, they were dragged through the mud, but they usually come out clean as a whistle."

"Their deliverable is a detailed description of each of their outcomes, including the process flowchart, impacted job roles and the tasks those job roles contribute to the overall process, the tools, equipment, facility and information required to produce the outcome. In fact, they are creating the Operations Blueprint I mentioned earlier.

Don't Cut Corners on the Operations Blueprint

"It is important that you force them to spend the time to get this right. Without a detailed analysis of the job tasks, and the tools, equipment, training, and job aids required for optimal performance, there is no way to determine what gaps exist, and what new capabilities you must establish in order to operate in the new model.

"The detailed performance requirements they will create are critical, because they will become the standard measure for accountability for change. During change implementation, it is common for resistors to smile and nod and say that they are doing things the new way without changing their behaviors at all. With detailed performance requirements you can both communicate your expectations and hold them accountable for making the change, because you have something quantifiable that you can measure against.

"Your Transformation Manager must ensure that the Implementation Teams use a standard method and tool for developing these detailed processes and procedures. This usually entails bringing in a trained facilitator to manage the closed-door workshops using a set of process design and gap analysis workshop templates.

"Be wary of the output and insist that it is done in a standard format across all the Implementation Teams. You must not allow them access to funds or resources for transformation activities until each team can prove that they have gone to the effort to do the analysis and produced a standard set of workshop deliverables."

For the first time in many minutes the king looked interested. "Frankly, Merlin, this is the stuff I like. Creating a new business model, designing the end-state organization and its processes. It's just about the only part of the process I actually enjoy."

V: Thou shalt design with the end in sight.

Keep the King Out of the Weeds

The wizard looked at him sharply. "Be aware, my king, you must not concern yourself too much with the details of processes or job-level procedures within the workforce. You must concern yourself with the strategic, with policies and the key outcomes of your business model."

"Don't worry, Merlin, I learned long ago the dangers of getting too far in the weeds," says Arthur. "To command an army, you must trust your commanders, just as they rely on their lieutenants, just as the lieutenants count on their captains and soldiers."

"Of course, Sire. This is one of the main reasons why you need a Transformation Manager and Implementation Teams. The Transformation Manager is your commander, and the Implementation Teams are his lieutenants and captains. It is their job to get into the weeds, just as it is your job to rise above them and survey the lay of the land."

Arthur sighed. "You know, Merlin, so far you've described an enormous amount of planning and design work that must be accomplished before actually kicking off the transformation itself." He waved off the wizard's objections. "Yes, yes, I know you told me that we shouldn't start the transformation itself until we have a detailed blueprint, plan and budget. I understand and agree. Here's what troubles me. All of this seems overwhelming. All this planning and scheming. The expense of bringing people together from all over the kingdom for these workshops. How can I justify the effort?"

Merlin narrowed his eyes. "Arthur, the beauty of this approach is that all the hard work of transformation, all the tough decisions and judgment calls, all the team

V: Thou shalt design with the end in sight.

and relationship building, is already done before you start the very first item on your Transformation Project Plan. Yes, it's hard, and yes it is expensive, but it sets you up for success. And the price of operational failure can be much, much higher than the amount you invest in good transformation planning and management."

Arthur nods slowly. "That actually makes sense, wizard. Maybe you are worth your ridiculous consulting rate."

Merlin lowers his gaze demurely. "Just so, your Greatness."

Arthur ignores him. "One more thing troubles me. How can I keep my people, especially my restless knights, interested and involved throughout the whole process? The long duration of the transformation will give my enemies time to put obstacles along the path to transformation."

"Time to discuss Commandment Six," says Merlin.

VI: Thou shalt pick winnable battles and celebrate the victories.

𝕴n war, how do you maintain high morale in your army during a long campaign?" asks Merlin.

Arthur responds instantly. "Good food."

Merlin grimaces. "Always the kidder, your Highness, but we both know that there is something that improves the morale of an army even more than a hot meal and cold ale."

Arthur considers for a moment. "Winning a battle, of course—nothing improves morale more than a battlefield victory! It feeds the troops' sense of righteous purpose."

Merlin smiles agreement. "It is the same with a long and difficult business transformation. It can be very hard for your organization to maintain the energy level required to endure change over long periods. You must sustain the passion in your workforce, especially your change agents. Just as in a long war, the best way to maintain morale is to produce a steady and continuous string of victories."

Win Early, Win Often, and Always Win

The wizard continues. "Part of your communications strategy must be to demonstrate a relentless series of successes to your stakeholders and the workforce, even if you have to create artificial milestones."

"Artificial milestones? That smacks of being unethical and anti-chivalrous," said the king.

"Don't be silly, Your Grace, it's just good project management and communications planning. In business transformation nothing is easy. Some things are hard, many are very hard, and some are well-nigh impossible. It's not unethical to start by picking the low-hanging fruit. Plan a series of initial low-risk wins that you can publicly celebrate early in the process. It is your duty to engineer the situation so you can ensure success. Think of what is at stake here."

Arthur ponders Merlin's words. "I could arrange a public event where we unveil the design for the round table, and reward the designer with a clutch of silver."

The wizard clapped his hands. "A perfect start, your Majesty. Then, a couple of weeks later, you could announce that an agreement has been reached with the Merchant's Guild to standardize wheat prices across the kingdom."

"But that's not a big deal, we negotiated that agreement a month ago."

"You're missing the point, Sire. Nobody knows about it. Make it a big deal! Write a press release! Spin it into a transformation success! Recognize the noble who negotiated the arrangement at next week's feast, and point out how his actions are aligned with your vision. From this moment forward you must be actively engineering outcomes that you can characterize as a transformation milestone. Use these accomplishments as a tool to convince others that it is in their personal interest to support your Cornerstones. "

VI: Thou shalt pick winnable battles and celebrate the victories.

Demonstrate Relentless Progress

"As I said in Commandment Four, the most effective approach for a communications strategy isn't a message; it's demonstrable success. Every month, you need to be making a speech, claiming victory over another milestone reached, another key capability established, and recognizing those who made it happen.

"Work with your Transformation Manager to devise your transformation timeline so that you can celebrate and reward successes on a regular basis. Think about it; wouldn't it be helpful if you could announce a victory, even a small one, at every monthly meeting of the Council of Knights or the bi-weekly meeting of the Bishop's Forum?

"This relentless messaging will show your commitment, and it demonstrates the success of your approach to the doubters. *A continuous series of regular successes publicly celebrated is critical to maintain the momentum of a business transformation initiative.*"

Publicly Celebrate Every Success

"You, Sire, must not claim credit, you must create a transformation environment where the knight or the merchant or even the lowest peasant can get meaningful reward and recognition for supporting the transformation. Focus on strengthening your champions and change agents, shower them with large praise and small tributes. You may also find opportunities to engage and reward influential bystanders, such as the archbishop. Take the opportunity! Anytime you can turn a bystander into a supporter you've moved one step closer to ultimate success."

VI: Thou shalt pick winnable battles and celebrate the victories.

Separate the Easy from the Hard

Merlin stopped pacing and faced the king. "What do you think is your most difficult challenge to transformation success?"

Arthur sighed. "No doubt it will be persuading my knights to accept the new organizational structures and command chains. In order to enforce equality, I may have to redistribute landholdings between the knights. Never before has this been done without resorting to war and bloodshed."

Merlin nods. "Yes, change at the top of an organization is usually politically-charged. You are dealing with powerful people in influential positions. You must move slowly and deliberately to avoid losing the support of the necessary leaders."

"Frankly, Merlin, I don't see how it can be done. And yet my vision depends on it." Arthur pounds his fists on his desk. "I will have to force them, somehow, to bend to my will. This single issue is the dragon I must slay to save my kingdom."

Merlin's voice is soothing. "Do not despair, my king. One of the tricks of business transformation is to separate the hard from the easy. You can make great progress towards your vision *without* reorganizing your knights.

"Remember this: *do not make the success of your overall effort dependent on an unachievable outcome.* If you do, you guarantee failure of the entire initiative. Instead, guarantee success by identifying these problematic outcomes and cordoning them off into their own areas of your transformation strategy so they do not jeopardize the success of the rest of the transformation."

VI: Thou shalt pick winnable battles and celebrate the victories.

Arthur looks doubtful. "But if these difficult changes are not accomplished, all else will be, ultimately, to no avail. The dragon will still threaten the kingdom."

"In my experience, Sire, you will find that as perceptions shift over the course of the transformation, what seemed impossible at the start may begin to seem more plausible. As the small wins pile up, you will reach a tipping point where the mass of the organization is behind you. This gives you tremendous power you can wield to solve problems that once seemed intractable. With your kingdom behind you, you may find it much easier to slay the dragon."

"So for the time being I should just ignore the dragon and leave the hard things to chance?"

Merlin chuckled. "No, no. You will be using your kingly influence all along to subtly influence the difficult issues. Work them in the background, and only announce your intentions publicly when you are confident that you will be successful. Do not tell your subjects you are going to slay the dragon until you are assured of victory."

Try to Avoid Public Executions, But Use Them When Necessary

Arthur shook his head, unconvinced. "I am certain that no matter how hard I try, there are people in high places that I will never win over to my side. Percy, for sure, and probably the master of the Merchant's Guild. Plus there are likely other resistors scattered throughout the kingdom that will make their presence known during the change effort."

Merlin sits down in his chair, reaches for the mug of mead, and drains the last few ounces. He wipes his beard with the cuff of his robe. "If a leading resistor can't

VI: Thou shalt pick winnable battles and celebrate the victories.

be marginalized..." He pauses, and then starts over. "You've tried convincing them to change, tried coercing them, tried everything in your power to make them see the light, but have failed... well, sometimes you have to sack them.

"Used extremely sparingly and very carefully, a quiet firing can send a shockwave through the workforce that has more impact than a hundred public celebrations. It can show your commitment to the future, and that you are serious in your pursuit of progress and of supporting your champions. It is the 'stick' to the many 'carrots' you have offered."

"I don't like that idea very much," Arthur replied. "It seems unchivalrous, plus it can have unintended consequences and backfire."

Merlin shakes his head. "Unchivalrous? No, quite the opposite. You owe it to those who are working hard for you to move intractable obstacles out of their way. But be very careful. Do it quietly. Don't shout from the rooftops. Believe me, it will be noticed.

Converting a Powerful Resistor is the Best Possible Victory

"Of course, converting a strong resistor sends a far more powerful message than sacking him. An opponent who sees the light and publicly switches sides is the most powerful tool in your toolbox, a public-relations coup. He or she will drag their followers along; plus, the bystanders will sit up and take notice. So, sack resistors only as a last resort."

"If I could only convert Percy, or his dreadful lieutenant Mordred... the lesser knights who follow them would certainly become supporters."

VI: Thou shalt pick winnable battles and celebrate the victories.

"As would the merchant guild," agrees Merlin.

"It will be hard."

"Yes, Sire, but that is why you and I make the big bucks. If it were easy, everyone would be doing it."

Arthur eyes the wizard. "We need a plan."

"The very subject of Commandment Seven," says Merlin.

VII: Thou shalt create and follow a transformation roadmap.

L ets review," says Merlin, stretching his feet out in front of his chair and leaning back to stare at the ceiling of Arthur's office. He ignores Arthur's sigh of protest, and drones on. "A builder needs two things to construct a castle: a *blueprint* that indicates the construction drawings of the finished structure, and a *project plan* that shows the activities and resources required to build the castle. It is the same in a business transformation initiative. Alongside your Operations Blueprint, you must have a Transformation Plan.

"We've talked about the Operations Blueprint in Commandment Five. In your Blueprint you will specify the key operational outcomes that your transformed business model will produce. The blueprint is a document that clearly communicates the to-be end state of your transformed business. It describes the detailed operations of your new model, including org charts, processes, procedures, job descriptions, and supporting technology.

"Enough, Merlin!" shouts Arthur. "I get it. I know what a blueprint is, and why it is important. Move along, please!"

Merlin clears his throat and sits up straight in his chair. "Yes, My Lord, of course. Now, where was I? Oh, yes. In order to build the transformed organization that your blueprint describes, you will need a Transformation Plan that communicates the construction approach, shows how to build it, who is accountable for getting it done, and what resources it will take."

VII: Thou shalt create and follow a transformation roadmap.

Three Building Blocks of the Transformation Plan

"The Transformation Plan has three building blocks that describe the objectives, the strategy, and the detailed process of transformation. They are:

1. The Cornerstone Objectives,
2. The Capability Development Roadmap, and
3. The Transformation Master Schedule.

"We discussed the first building block, the Transformation Cornerstone Objectives, in Commandment One; they provide high-level requirements and guidance for the overall plan. The second building block, the Capability Development Roadmap, indicates the strategies and intermediate milestones for achieving the Cornerstone Objectives. The third building block, the Transformation Master Schedule, provides the detailed, day-by-day project management plan to accomplish the milestones on the Roadmap."

"Designing the Transformation Plan using these three building blocks makes it possible to trace every resource expended on the Master Schedule back through the Roadmap and all the way to a Cornerstone Objective. This is important, because it enables the Transformation Manager to ensure that every single penny spent on transformation is contributing to the achievement of a Cornerstone Objective."

"You're talking about requirements traceability," says Arthur.

Merlin looks up with raised eyebrows. "Why, yes, Majesty. Exactly."

VII: Thou shalt create and follow a transformation roadmap.

Arthur snorts. "Don't look so surprised, wizard. Like I said earlier, you don't get to be king without knowing a few things about business."

Merlin bows his head. "It is a pleasure to be in the company of a kindred intellect, my Liege."

Arthur rolls his eyes at Merlin's obsequiousness. "Okay, so explain to me the reason behind breaking the Transformation Plan into these three components. Why not simply create the detailed project plan? After all, that's what you will need to create the budget and administer the transformation."

"A perceptive question," says Merlin. "The three components of the Transformation Plan are targeted toward three different audiences and have three different purposes.

Cornerstone Objectives

"The Cornerstone Objectives are intended to be understood by the entire kingdom. They are stated in simple terms and represent a call-to-action that everyone from a peasant to a knight can understand. Achieving a Cornerstone objective is cause for a major, kingdom-wide celebration.

Capability Development Roadmap

"The Capability Development Roadmap is more detailed. It is targeted at the senior leadership, your key stakeholders, and your change agents. It shows the overall strategy and timeline for the transformation, and most importantly, the intermediate milestones along the way. It is more of a communications and alignment tool for your key leaders than a project management tool. Achieving a Roadmap milestone is another opportunity for celebration and recognition of those who made it possible.

Transformation Master Schedule

"The Roadmap serves a further purpose; it is the guiding resource that your Transformation Manager and Implementation Teams will use to guide them as they produce the detailed Master Schedule. The tasks on the master schedule must comply with the timeline and milestones of the Roadmap."

"That's actually quite clever," says Arthur. "Instead of watching my deputy's eyes glaze over while I try to talk for an hour about a detailed project plan, I can instead review the high-level roadmap in less than five minutes. And when I address the townsfolk and farmers, I can speak in the simple terms of the Cornerstone Objectives."

"Precisely," agrees Merlin. "These tools play a bigger role than just project management. They are also key elements of your communications strategy to promote education and awareness of the change, and to set expectations for action."

The Roadmap is the Centerpiece of the Transformation Plan

Merlin picks up the slate and wipes it clean with his cuff. White soapstone dust from the repeated cleanings soils the wizard's expensive black robe. Merlin, in his excitement, ignores the mess, and scratches at the slate for a few minutes.

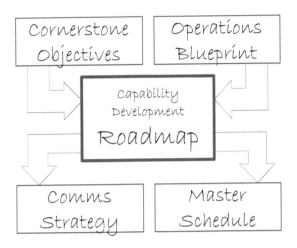

He hands the slate to Arthur. "The Capability Development Roadmap ties all the elements of the change management methodology together; it is the centerpiece of your Transformation Plan. It shows the path toward attaining the Cornerstone Objectives by *defining the capability-development activities required to enable the key outcomes from the Operations Blueprint.*"

"It provides the basis for the detailed Master Schedule. It also provides fodder for your Communications Plan—the steady stream of milestones gives you a vehicle for regular public celebrations of success as we discussed in Commandment Six."

"I'm having a hard time visualizing it. What does a Roadmap look like?" Arthur asks.

Merlin attacks the slate yet again. "Here you go, your Highness."

VII: Thou shalt create and follow a transformation roadmap.

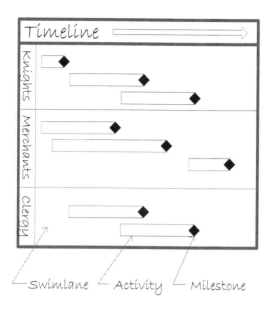

"As you can see, the Roadmap shows high-level capability-development activities along a timeline, grouped in swimlanes, and indicates major milestones. It provides an easy way for you to communicate your entire plan in five minutes or less, and shows how you will achieve your vision. It is not a detailed project plan, though it does inform the detailed Master Schedule. It is the guiding strategic document that shows priorities for action and resource allocation."

Arthur holds the slate carefully, trying not to get any of the white soapstone powder on his hands. "I see the milestones are regularly-spaced along the timeline. Are those the continual wins of which you spoke?"

"Yes, Sire. A good Roadmap will incorporate all of the change management concepts we've discussed. When we design your Roadmap, we will prioritize your activities to create early wins to build early momentum. We will continue the momentum by engineering milestones along

VII: Thou shalt create and follow a transformation roadmap.

the timeline so that you can celebrate continual wins and enjoy a steady stream of rewards and recognitions for your key change agents. We will tie milestones to the achievement of key operational outcomes from your blueprint. And everything on the Roadmap will relentlessly push toward the attainment of the Cornerstone Objectives."

Arthur nodded, clearly impressed. "Ah, I understand. This is not the battle plan, but the overarching war plan."

"Exactly, your Majesty."

Arthur continues to study the slate. "I see that you've set up swimlanes by organizational unit."

"Organizational swimlanes are very useful; they show each business unit what is expected of it, and how its activities relate to and support the activities of other groups. Your Roadmap will likely also have functional swimlanes for key cross-cutting activities, such as shared technology implementation and enterprise policy development."

"The swimlanes will show how important it is to have a coordinated approach to transformation. Many business transformation initiatives waste enormous resources when certain elements get out ahead of others, and then collapse because the infrastructure they needed had not yet been built.

"Think of your kingdom as a three-legged stool, and the goal of your transformation project is to increase the height of the stool.

"Your key operational outcomes are marbles sitting on top of the stool. If you unbalance the stool at any point during the transformation, some marbles will roll off and your operations will be jeopardized. The roadmap shows how you will coordinate the lengthening of each leg in such a manner as to keep the stool level the entire time. In other words, Your Greatness, the roadmap keeps you from losing your marbles."

Roadmap Focus Factors

"Not all capability development activities are created equal. Some are easier or more difficult, some are political landmines or time bombs, and some will have far more impact than others, so you should craft the grouping and sequence carefully."

Arthur handed the slate back to Merlin. "Just as in war," he said, "Some battles are quick strikes, others are long arduous sieges. Both require planning. In war planning you want some quick strike victories up front to build morale for the long sieges to come." He lowered his voice. "Dealing with Percy will be a siege. Reorganizing the knights' hierarchy and landholdings will be a siege. I have to tell you, wizard, my greatest fear is that I won't be able to slay these particular dragons, no matter what else I do."

Don't Let the Lurking Dragons Spoil the Day

Merlin lowered his voice to match Arthur. "Some things are so politically sensitive, so potentially disrupting, that they must be purposefully omitted from the roadmap, to be resolved in a separate continuum so they do not destroy the transformation effort before it can begin.

"You have said that reorganizing the knights' landholdings will be as difficult as slaying a dragon. If you make the reorganization a cornerstone objective and display the process on the roadmap, you may ignite such a

VII: Thou shalt create and follow a transformation roadmap.

furor from the powerful knights that the whole business transformation effort collapses. You must not tie the success of the transformation to the slaying of the dragon, even if it means you have to de-scope your overall expectations.

"One useful strategy for mitigating the risks associated with dragon-sized challenges is to disconnect them completely from the business transformation and encapsulate them in another, discrete initiative. Even though you may manage them as one effort internally, you must split the dragon from the rest of the transformation, so that if you are not successful in eventually slaying it, all is not lost."

Arthur contemplates the wizard's advice. "Well, maybe we can keep the dragon at bay for a while, but we still have to deal with the Devil himself."

Merlin looks uncertain. "The Devil, my lord?"

Arthur chuckles. "Haven't you heard the saying that the Devil is in the details?"

Merlin shrugs, obviously not happy that the king is using humor instead of himself. "Yes, I have heard the saying."

Merlin's discomfort makes Arthur's smile widen. "Oh, come on, wizard, you mentioned the Transformation Master Schedule several times. I take it that it contains the details in which the Devil lives?"

"Yes, your Grace," Merlin pouts, "and it is the subject of Commandment Eight."

VII: Thou shalt create and follow a transformation roadmap.

VIII: Thou shalt know
the resources required
for transformation.

$\mathfrak{T}$he devil is in the details," repeats Merlin. "And it's in the details where most business transformations falter. Hence this commandment is dedicated to the home of the devil, the Transformation Master Schedule.

"You said yourself, my Liege, the Capability Development Roadmap we discussed in Commandment Seven is your overarching strategic war plan, but it doesn't contain enough tactical detail to be of use by the soldiers on the ground. This is where the Transformation Master Schedule comes in; it comprises your detailed battle plans."

Transformation Resource Management

Merlin stands up and once again proceeds to pace, hands behind his back. "On the battlefield, when two armies of equal number and skill meet, what determines the victor?"

Arthur didn't hesitate. "The supply line."

Merlin nods. "And so it is with business transformation. Just as you cannot win a battle without careful resource management, neither can you transform an organization.

"In order to know what resources are required on the battlefield, you need a detailed battle plan to ascertain how many soldiers you'll need, and what arms, food, shelter, transportation, engineering equipment they require.

"Knowing these requirements and reconciling them with your budget is critical. There will never be enough resources, so you will be forced to make tradeoffs. With a detailed battle plan, you can make those tradeoffs in the most optimal manner, long before you meet the enemy. This is far better than discovering that you've run out of resources during the heat of the battle.

"The Transformation Manager owns the battle plans, the Master Schedule, for your business transformation. He develops them in concert with the Implementation Teams, who are accountable for their execution. The Transformation Manager tracks the Master Schedule, while each Implementation Team leader tracks his or her subsection of the plan.

Transformation Management vs. Operations Management

"Let's clear up one common area of confusion. The Transformation Master Schedule is not the same thing as your ongoing operations management plan. It will necessarily impact your operations management plan as new capabilities are established and old one decommissioned, but where your operations plan describes a steady state ongoing operation, the transformation plan has a beginning and an end. When it is complete, the transformation is over, and you are operating in the new, fully-transformed model."

Building the Capabilities to Implement the Operations Blueprint

"Remember the key operational outcomes that are the heart your Operations Blueprint? Standing up the capability to implement these operational outcomes is the primary purpose of the Master Schedule.

VIII: Thou shalt know the resources required for transformation.

76

Arthur raises his hand. "Hold on - I'm lost here. What exactly does that mean?"

"It might help if I define the word *capability*. In the context of business transformation, a capability can be one of any number of things that must be put in place before you can implement a new business process. These can include new job skills, updated policies and processes, new tools or technology, and new administrative infrastructure. All these things are called capabilities, and the work required to stand up each capability must be included as a task on your Transformation Master Schedule.

"Simply speaking, the Master Schedule is the project plan to close the capability gaps between your 'as-is' business model and the 'to-be' model you designed in your Operations Blueprint.

"It must show the capability development tasks, and clearly indicate who is accountable for the task accomplishment. Just as importantly, it must show the resources required to complete the task successfully."

"Give me an example," says Arthur.

"Certainly, your Highness." Merlin thinks for a moment. "One of your cornerstones is 'Equal justice for all subjects.' Let's say that in your Operations Blueprint you have a key operational outcome that supports this cornerstone, and it is called 'Fair Trial by a Jury of Peers.'

"In your current business model, each knight holds court, and without much oversight he makes judgment for crimes committed within his barony. In order to build the capability for a jury trial standard across the land, your Implementation Teams will be forced to manage a carefully-planned series of tasks to close the gaps between the way it is done now, and the way it is designed in your Blueprint.

"For example, they will need to develop new policies for the conduct of trials and the selection of judges and jurors. They will need to develop and deliver training to the new judges. There will need to be some system to manage the scheduling of trials, and some way to track the administrative paperwork associated with the whole enterprise. You may need to build a courthouse. All of these activities take time and cost money. You need to know how long, and how much, so you can make budget decisions and set priorities. The process of creating the Master Schedule gives you this information."

Arthur buries his face in his hands. "I'm already starting to see the Devil in these details, Merlin. There could be thousands of capability-development tasks that are required to fully realize my vision."

Merlin sighs. "Yes, Arthur, but with the Roadmap and Master Schedule, you have a fighting chance of success, whereas without them, you leave the implementation of your vision to chance.

"Also keep in mind that while there may be myriad tasks to complete, you have a large workforce at your disposal. The whole idea of the Implementation Teams is designed to give you the resources to manage the details, and keep the Devil out of your hair."

Budgeting for Transformation

"As king, you don't need to know the details of the Master Schedule, but you do need to know what the transformation project is going to cost your treasury. By knowing the cost of the tasks required to stand up new capabilities and decommission old capabilities, you will

VIII: Thou shalt know the resources required for transformation.

know what impact the transformation will have to your capital and operational budgets and cashflows.

"Keep in mind that transformation costs as determined by the Master Schedule are *in addition to* the ongoing operational expenses of your enterprise. While the transformation may impact the costs of operation, they must be accounted for separately. In this manner you can compare the projected costs of transformation to the financial and performance benefits of the new business model to see if the transformation is worth pursuing.

Arthur grunts. "Hopefully the increased operational productivity and decreased costs due to efficiency gains will more than offset the costs of transformation."

Merlin smiles. "That's the idea, Your Highness, but without going through the detailed planning, you'll never know for sure."

"So how does it work?" asks the king.

"Your Transformation Manager will map the key capability-development activities along the Roadmap timeline. He will sequence them according to the priorities of the Roadmap, and then as precedence dictates due to dependencies on other activities being completed first.

"Then, working backwards, and with the assistance of the Implementation Teams, he will determine the tasks and resources required to achieve the capabilities. In this way you will have some idea of what resources, human or otherwise, are required to be successful, and can scope and scale your plans accordingly.

VIII: Thou shalt know the resources required for transformation.

Initial and Intermediate States

"Another benefit of the detailed Master Schedule is that it can uncover risks and issues that would remain hidden at higher levels. Building the Roadmap and Master Schedule is an iterative process. You create them at the same time, and one informs the other.

"For complex, multi-year transformations like yours, it may be useful to chunk up the Roadmap and Master Schedule into phases, or even better, what I call 'capability states.' For example, you might want to define intermediate capability states, such as 'Initial Operating Capability' or "Intermediate Operating Capability.' Achieving these states gives you one more thing to celebrate and communicate, plus it can make management of the transformation plan easier for your implementation teams because it enables them to chunk the work into manageable bits."

Flexibility and the Change Control Board

"There is such a thing as too much planning," says Arthur. "One of the first axioms of warfare is that no plan survives first contact with the enemy. Flexibility and adaptability are critical to winning any battle."

"This is where your Transformation Manager will prove his worth," replies Merlin. "His job is to push the implementation of the plan, identify and manage risks before they turn into issues, and modify the plans and resource allocations to keep progress toward major milestones.

"The best way to manage the inevitable changes to your Roadmap and Master Schedule is to establish a Change Control Board. The board is established as soon as the initial versions of the Blueprint, Roadmap, and

VIII: Thou shalt know the resources required for transformation.

Master Schedule are completed. At that point, all three documents become subject to version control and a change review-and-approval process. Any change to the Master Schedule that impacts the Roadmap requires approval by the Change Control Board. Also, any change to the Blueprint that impacts the definition of a key operational outcome is also subject to review and approval.

"The Change Control Board acts like a supreme court; its role is to protect the intent of the Cornerstones and Cornerstone Objectives, and not to allow a deviation that would violate these guiding principles.

"Note that the board does not review minor changes to either the Master Schedule or the Blueprint. Only significant changes, at the level of an operational outcome or a Roadmap activity warrant the attention of the board. Minor changes can be made by the Transformation Manager working with the appropriate Implementation Teams.

"The Change Control Board must meet regularly and act swiftly on decisions so that they do not impede the progress of the transformation."

"This board will have much power," observes Arthur. "How can I assure that the board follows my wishes and makes decisions that are aligned with my vision?"

Merlin smiles. "Because you, Sire, will be the chairman of the Change Control Board. In fact, it is one of the most important roles you will play during the implementation phases of transformation."

Establish Accountability for Change

"The Master Schedule also has great value because it establishes individual accountability for every single task in the transformation plan. Every task has a person's name assigned to it, and it is that person's responsibility to ensure that the task gets done."

"Ah, so I can recognize and reward those who are achieving success, and discipline those who are dragging their feet."

"Exactly! In fact, this accountability is most effective when you include it in every employee's annual performance evaluation. For example, you can include standard language in everyone's job description that says they will be graded on how well they perform their assigned tasks in the Transformation Master Schedule. This gives each individual employee a personal stake in the success of the transformation.

"You must place even stronger language in the job descriptions of key transformation roles, such as the Transformation Manager or members of your Implementation Teams. These roles are critical to the success of your transformation and greatly impact the design and implementation of the Blueprint, Roadmap and Master Schedule.

Arthur shakes his head, as if to clear the cobwebs. "You've talked a lot about these roles, but I'm still not clear on them. Who, exactly, does what?"

"Here's how the accountability stacks up for the key transformation management roles.

Role of the King

"You, Sire, are responsible for spreading the word and making sure that everyone in the kingdom knows your vision for the future and can recite the Transformation Cornerstones. You are also responsible for resolving conflicts that occur between the executive leadership of the organization, especially those conflicts that occur at a level where neither the Change Manager nor the Implementation Teams have the authority to intervene. You act as the chair of the Change Management Board and have the final approval authority for any significant proposed deviations to the Roadmap or Blueprint."

Role of the Change Manager

"Your Change Manager is responsible for guiding the organization through the change management methodology, including establishing the Implementation Teams, facilitating the creation of the Cornerstone Objectives and Communications Plan, and overseeing the creation of the Blueprint, Roadmap, and Master Schedule. During implementation of the transformation plan, he or she will monitor the progress of the Implementation Teams and identify and resolve issues and risks encountered along the way. The Change Manager will also participate on the Change Control Board, where modifications to the Blueprint or Plan will be reviewed.

Role of the Implementation Teams

"The Implementation Teams provide the subject matter expertise and the 'boots-on-the-ground' resources to manage the details of the plan. The team leader owns a discrete section of the Master Schedule that is related to his organization or functional area. He or she is responsible for the creation of that section of the Master Schedule, as well as the management of that section's tasks and resources during the implementation period. The team lead is responsible for identifying risks and reporting them to the Change Manager before they become issues. Members of the Implementation Teams may be called to participate on the Change Control Board when the proposed change concerns their organizational unit or functional area of expertise.

Role of the Employee

"Each member of the workforce also has a role to play, as any member may be assigned a transformation-related task according to the Master Schedule. Supervisors must allocate time and resources as required to enable the employee to complete the task, and carefully manage the work portfolio so that it minimizes impact to the ongoing operational processes.

Arthur shakes his head slowly. "Merlin, this change model you describe is daunting in its complexity and difficulty. Not only do I have to design and develop countless data points including new policies, organizational processes, job procedures and operational metrics, but I also have to manage a complex transformation plan. You have to admit it sounds completely overwhelming."

For the first time since entering Arthur's office, Merlin's cynical expression completely vanished. He leaned forward toward the king. "My king, you are absolutely correct. Now you know why eight out of ten large-scale business transformation efforts fail. It IS daunting and incredibly complex.

"But do not despair. The twenty percent that succeed are the ones that recognize, as you have, that business transformation is the most difficult task you will ever face as a leader. The leaders who are successful in enterprise wide change have all found a way to manage the transformation process and have employed each of the Ten Commandments to do so.

VIII: Thou shalt know the resources required for transformation.

The sly smile crept its way back on Merlin's face. "You, Sire, are lucky in that you have a fighting chance to succeed."

"And why, pray tell, is that?"

Merlin shrugs. "Because you have me!"

Arthur scowls, but then sighs and smiles. "Wizard you are insufferable!"

"It's hard to be modest when you are a consultant to the king," the wizard agrees. "But enough about me. Let's address your concern about managing the incredible complexity of an enterprise-wide business transformation."

"Commandment Nine?" asks Arthur.

"Commandment Nine," agrees Merlin.

VIII: Thou shalt know the resources required for transformation.

IX: Thou shalt have systems to manage volumes of data and complexity.

*L*et's summarize the information and data that your Transformation Manager will need to track during a large-scale business transformation initiative." Merlin spent a few minutes scribbling noisily on the slate, then handed it to the king.

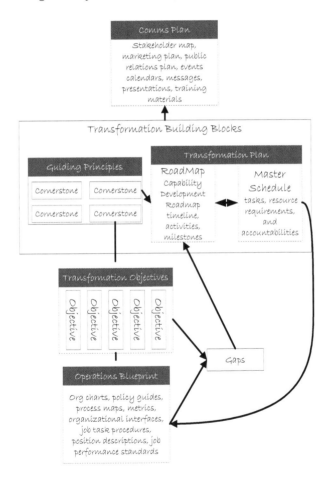

IX: Thou shalt have systems to manage volumes of data and complexity.

Arthur studied the diagram. "That's a lot of moving parts."

Merlin nodded. "To make it worse, they are all interconnected and must be managed as an integrated system. In many ways, business transformation is a lot like changing the wheel of a Roman chariot while the chariot is charging into battle. You must find a way to change the wheel without slowing or overturning the chariot or ejecting its occupants."

"In other words, it's impossible."

"No, not impossible—it just takes a lot of planning, special tools, and intense coordinated efforts during the actual implementation. And, I'll admit, a little good luck."

Arthur tossed the slate on his desk and gestured at it. "So how do I manage all this complexity, all these interconnected concepts and methods and procedures and tools, without wrecking my chariot in the process?"

Information Management Strategy

"A multi-year business transformation involving a workforce of hundreds or thousands of employees requires careful attention to detail and entails managing hundreds of thousands of data points. No large-scale transformation can succeed without a strategy to manage all this important information.

"Your Transformation Manager will need to work with your Chief Information Officer to develop the information management resources required to administer a project of this magnitude. At minimum, you'll need a system to track changes to the enterprise architecture, a system to manage all the new and revised documentation and publications, a system to manage

IX: Thou shalt have systems to manage volumes of data and complexity.

workforce competencies and learning, and a project management system to track the tasks in the Master Schedule and manage risks and issues."

Enterprise Architecture System

"Your Operations Blueprint will contain a large amount of process and procedural information, such as process descriptions, procedures, and flowcharts, and all the associated business process data. Depending on the configuration and policies of your existing enterprise architecture system, you may be able to use it during the planning phases to document the proposed 'to-be' business model. Most likely, however, you'll need a separate database to manage the proposed business process changes until the new processes are actually implemented.

"Once the changes in your Operations Blueprint are implemented, they will likely impact several components of your existing enterprise architecture. Each key operational outcome in the Blueprint may dictate a change to one or more enterprise architecture frameworks, as well as potential changes to data and processes in the financial, asset, facility, and human resources management systems. The resources required to update these systems must be factored in to the costs and timeline of transformation.

Document Management/Knowledge Management System

"Think about the sheer volume of new and revised documentation that may be required to implement large-scale change across the kingdom. New or updated policy guides, process guides, and standard operating

IX: Thou shalt have systems to manage volumes of data and complexity.

procedures. Also technical manuals, desk guides, position descriptions and job aids.

"Because all of these documents must support the Operations Blueprint, you need some method to manage the update and review process. Your Implementation Teams will be critical in this role, but they can effectively manage the complexity of the task only with a document management system of some kind that will help them share documents while maintaining version control.

Learning Management System

"The Implementation Teams will also face the challenge of establishing new competencies in the workforce. New training programs will need to be developed and delivered to targeted groups of workers.

"Learning management poses several unique challenges during business transformation. Once a training needs assessment is complete, the Implementation Teams must oversee the development of courses and job aids for the targeted job roles. Each course will probably have some type of test or evaluation process to ensure that learning has occurred. Finally, there must be some system in place to track the individual employee's progress in gaining the required competencies."

"Fortunately, there are specialized information management systems designed for just these tasks. They are known and Learning Management Systems, and they are usually comprised of a system to manage content development, and a system to track employee progress.

IX: Thou shalt have systems to manage volumes of data and complexity.

Project Management System

"You'll need a robust project management system that your Transformation Manager can use to create and administer the Transformation Master Schedule, as well as track and manage risks and issues.

Finally, you'll need a method to communicate transformation progress, risks, success and accountability to all stakeholders in the transformation. Which brings us at last to Commandment Ten."

IX: Thou shalt have systems to manage volumes of data and complexity.

X: Thou shalt measure and communicate progress, risk, and accountability.

It's important to know what success looks like; otherwise, how will you know when you've successfully completed transformation? With your Cornerstones and Objectives, you've defined the success factors. With the Operations Blueprint, you've driven the end-state vision down to the individual job level. With the Capability Development Roadmap and the Master Schedule you've identified the tasking and milestones that will be celebrated along the way.

"All these things are good and necessary, but taken together they represent a mass of information that no single individual can fully grasp. Furthermore, with a large, multi-year program, the transformation can lose steam. Key players will shift, and new faces will enter the mix. How will you continue to light the path to the future so that they remain motivated and aligned with your original vision of success?

Arthur shrugs at the wizard's question. "I suppose you're about to tell me."

Merlin ignores the king's cynical tone and continues his monologue. "The answer is to institutionalize the change process itself so that performing the change-related activities on the Master Schedule is a normal and expected part of everyone's job. For this strategy to work, however, you and your Transformation Manager must have an unprecedented level of visibility and control over the transformation

X: Thou shalt measure and communicate progress, risk, and accountability.

activities, and be able to communicate the details to every single impacted employee."

Transformation Command Center

"In order to get the big picture of the current status and future direction of the overall transformation initiative, you need a tool to consolidate all the information into a single place. I call this tool the Transformation Command Center.

"That sounds important," says Arthur.

"You are correct. The purpose of the Command Center is to provide centralized visibility into the decentralized activities taking place at many levels within your organization. Because of the layers of complexity it can be very hard to visualize the progress and current state of the transformation at any one point in time.

"The Command Center helps the Transformation Manager and the Implementation Teams answer many important questions. How are we doing? What course corrections do we need to make? What's the best place to spend our next transformation dollar? What are the most pressing risks? Who deserves reward for great progress, and who deserves discipline for dragging their feet? What is the next milestone to celebrate?"

Measure Progress toward Transformation Milestones

"In order to implement the Command Center, I will use sorcery called the Internet and the World Wide Web, along with a magical tool called a software dashboard. It will enable anyone in the kingdom to access the Command Center, and see the overall progress of the transformation, and drill down into their specific areas to see what is expected of them."

X: Thou shalt measure and communicate progress, risk, and accountability.

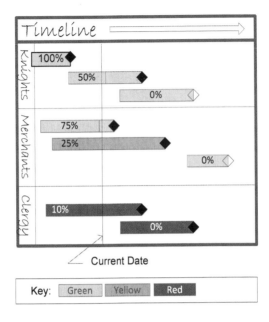

"At the highest level, the Command Center must be able to depict the organization's aggregate progress toward the Transformation Cornerstones. From there the user can drill down to view progress toward each Cornerstone Objective, and from there they can continue to drill down to view progress toward Roadmap activities and milestones. In this way the casual user can discover how each lower level contributes to the overall progress toward higher-level objectives. This understanding and awareness is an important benefit of the Command Center because it enables each individual to see how their own personal activities are contributing to the overall progress.

Enforce Accountability for Correct Change

"There is a common phenomenon in change management. It goes something like this: you task an organization or an individual to make a change, give them

---

X: Thou shalt measure and communicate progress, risk, and accountability.

the requirements, and they come back some time later with a glowing report that indicates success in adopting the new change. Only, nothing really changed.

"This can be caused by resistance, by laziness, or most likely by a misunderstanding of the requirements. No matter the cause, the result is the same; wasted time and money.

"The way to avoid this phenomenon is to create verification criteria for each transformation activity. These criteria must define clear and unambiguous measures of success for the activity. The accountable party must think of them as audit criteria, and should be prepared for an audit on the outcomes of the transformation activity. Indeed, it is a good practice for the Transformation Manager to routinely perform audits on critical activities.

"Trust but verify. A wise policy," agrees Arthur.

"Just so, your Eminence. Every activity and milestone on the Roadmap, and every summary task on the Master Schedule must have verification criteria, and an individual assigned to the task who is responsible for meeting the criteria. This person is accountable to the Transformation Manager for ensuring that the activity is completed on schedule and at the projected cost. The activity owner is also accountable for managing any risks or issues that are encountered.

Risks and Issue Management

"In addition to quantifying progress toward milestones, the Command Center also reports risks that may impact the schedule and issues that already have impacted the schedule. Knowledge of these two elements is critical to transformation management. They determine what corrective actions need to be done to get the schedule back on track, and depending on the severity of the risk or issue, where the next transformation dollar is spent.

"Each item on the Command Center must have a risk severity indicator of red, yellow, or green, depending on how much the Master Schedule might be impacted.

"A user of the Command Center must be able to select the risk indicator and see the activity owner's description of the risk or issue, along with their recommendations for resolving it.

Executive Transformation Management

"Here's the best part. You and I, Sire, will simply be able to glance at the Command Center, and where we see a high level of risk, drill down to discover the root cause of the problem. This makes it easy for us to focus on the items that represent a strategic threat to the transformation. We can efficiently manage just the exceptions, instead of being forced to constantly devote resources to monitoring the whole plan. If the entire dashboard is green, the transformation is flowing smoothly. If a risk indicator turns yellow or red, then we can quickly mobilize to resolve the potential problem and minimize the impact to the budget or schedule.

"There can be several causes of poor progress or increased risk. Perhaps the accountable individual isn't doing their job. Or, the problem may be caused by external influences not under the control of the activity owner. Either way, the Command Center makes it possible to minimize the effect or risk on the Master Schedule.

X: Thou shalt measure and communicate progress, risk, and accountability.

Communicate Cornerstone Progress to All Stakeholders

"You will get the most value out of the Command Center by using it as your primary communications tool during the transformation implementation phase. Every time you meet with your knights, or your staff, or any of the stakeholders, spend a few minutes showing the dashboard and discussing the progress, risks, and issues. Every time you address your subjects, or the Merchant Guild, or the clergy, show the dashboard and point to the progress being made.

"Each time the Transformation Manager meets with the Implementation Teams, the Command Center must guide their discussion. Whenever someone on the Implementation Team assigns a transformation task to an individual, they must show them how the task is being measured on the Command Center and how their personal performance will be visible to everyone up to and including the king himself.

"Eventually, everyone will turn to the Command Center on their own to see their own progress, their colleague's progress, and the overall progress of the entire organization.

Visibility Promotes Healthy Competition

"Soon you will begin to see an unexpected and welcome phenomenon. Competition will break out amongst the divisions within your enterprise. With everything publicly visible, nobody will want their section of the dashboard to show poor progress or high risk. You will see your executives and managers talking amongst themselves and sharing ideas on how to 'stay green.' 'This is one of the most powerful benefits of the Command

---

X: Thou shalt measure and communicate progress, risk, and accountability.

Center; it promotes beneficial competition and sharing of best practices across the enterprise.

Command Center Administration

"Establishing and operating the Command Center will require dedicated resources and commitment of key personnel throughout the life of the transformation project. It is the Transformation Manager's responsibility to set up and operate the dashboard, as well as provide training on its use.

"The Transformation Manager must designate a member of his staff as the Dashboard Administrator. This individual is tasked with establishing the underlying database (another bit of sorcery), entering the data from the Roadmap and Master Schedule, and updating the data when changes are approved by the Change Control Board.

"The Dashboard Administrator works with the Implementation Teams to keep the progress and risk data current. The Implementation Teams work with the Dashboard Administrator to coordinate regular updates, preferably every week. Because there may be dozens, even hundreds, of activity owners, it is important that the update process be streamlined and easy, and that reporting progress and risk be minimized."

Merlin stopped pacing and sat heavily in the seat facing the king's desk. He slapped his hands on the stone tablets with great finality. "And, that, Sire, is that. These are the Ten Commandments of Business Transformation. Disregard them at great peril."

X: Thou shalt measure and communicate progress, risk, and accountability.

Arthur looks out the window behind the now-silent wizard. The sun is sinking low on the horizon and the rays stream almost horizontally through the office. He marvels at the sudden silence; the wizard has been talking non-stop for hours. He clears his throat. "Are you done?"

Merlin nods solemnly. "It's been a long afternoon, Your Majesty. No doubt you will need some time to digest all this information."

"It's like a piece of tough, chewy meat," replies Arthur. "Destined to give me terrible indigestion."

Merlin smiles. "But a meal that is ultimately nourishing, my Liege." He narrows his eye at Arthur. "You didn't expect it would be easy, did you?"

Arthur sighs. "No, I guess not. I just didn't anticipate so many moving pieces."

"Nothing you will ever do will be more difficult as leading a multi-year, enterprise-wide change effort. But at least you are forewarned as to what to expect, and know the basics of what you'll need to be successful.

"Don't lose faith, Arthur. Your vision is sound, and it will herald a new era of peace and prosperity for your kingdom and all your subjects. Transformation is tough, but the effort is worth it."

He gestured at the stone tablets, now lit with the soft red glow of the setting sun. "Keep these for a while. When you are ready to begin, call me."

X: Thou shalt measure and communicate progress, risk, and accountability.

Epilogue: The Next
Few Years

erlin gave Arthur a lot to consider that first day, and his head started to hurt. He decided to go to bed early to get a good night's rest. As he lay in the royal bed, hundreds of thoughts ran through his mind.

This transformation process would not be easy, but it was the one thing that would save the kingdom, and enable his vision of Camelot. It had to be managed carefully, but on the other hand, he had to relinquish some of the control of the planning and execution to his knights and his subjects. Their involvement would create ownership, not just buy-in, and that was a key factor for success. He needed a plan to communicate this vision to the entire kingdom; one that would speak to different audiences at different levels of interest and involvement. And he had to sway knights like Percy to bring the entire kingdom together. Oh, and the mountains of data, how was he going to make sure everything got done? And how was he going to communicate progress and accountability, manage his resources, keep the project on track *and* go about the day-to-day business of running a kingdom?

"Thank God I have Merlin on my side." thought the king. "As much of a royal pain as he is, he is the only one who will keep me sane through this process."

Key Leader's Workshop

One of the first things that Merlin did was facilitate a one-day Key Leader's Workshop with King

Arthur and all of the knights. In the workshop the king presented the cornerstones of his vision:

1. Peerage among the knights
2. Equal justice for all subjects
3. The Code of Chivalry
4. Defense of Crown and Country

The cornerstones were met with general acceptance. Lancelot thought the whole plan was brilliant! All of the knights could certainly gather around the notions of Defense of Crown and Country, and The Code of Chivalry. Percy, however, was having some difficulty with cornerstones 1 and 2.

Percy remained quiet as he pondered the first cornerstone. He thought, "Peerage among the knights... I don't want peerage. I am personally at the top of this food chain and that's where I want to stay. The other knights look up to me because I know how to do everything." He moved on to the second cornerstone and thought, "Equal Justice? I keep my subjects in line. I need to rule my territory as I see fit. Equal justice, my Armor!"

Mordred, a knight with little power but a strong dislike for the king, observed Percy's obvious dislike for the proposed change and commiserated with Percy in the corner. Mordred brought other knights quietly into their conversation with hopes of gaining momentum on dissent.

Most of the knights rallied around the vision. They were eager to work together to create the remaining objectives that would support the vision. Merlin noticed the small, but growing, contingent in the corner and knew that he needed to attend to that before it took hold. It wasn't going to be easy, but turning Percy from "resistor" to "champion" was Merlin's first order of business. He couldn't be obvious, though his dislike for Percy was hard to conceal. And he had to play to Percy's strength of confidence. Merlin had a plan.

To minimize his involvement, Merlin assigned Mordred a clerical role that kept him very busy during the proceedings, but not in a key decision making role. Then, after lunch he teamed Percy with Sir Kay (whom he knew to be just, brave, and a friend to all the knights) and a few other knights to take a lead role in defining objectives for the 2nd cornerstone. By assigning Percy a key role, Merlin observed his need for importance and control. By teaming him with Sir Kay he assured that fairness would prevail.

Merlin knew that Percy needed to have his concerns be heard, and that Sir Kay would listen. He also knew that Sir Kay would not be swayed to pessimism and negativity, and would find, recognize and utilize Percy's strengths. In the end, Percy decided that maybe "Peerage among knights" could be beneficial, and that "Equal Justice for all subjects" was a cause definitely worth fighting for. He even contributed key points to the objectives and outcomes. Percy's position on the in the Stakeholder Matrix moved three spaces towards Champion and away from Resistor that day.

All of the knights worked together to create the new governance structure that would support the cornerstones. They developed Governance outcomes, assigned accountabilities, devised measures of success, came up with slogans to support the change, and began working on the nuts and bolts of the supporting processes.

Change Management Office

The decision was made to charter a Change Management Office, to be led by Sir Galahad working in close concert with Merlin. Along with a few analysts and technical writers, they would oversee the transformation. Arthur made a big deal out of the new office, announcing its charter at the Spring feast at Camelot.

Percy, King Pellinore, Sir Kay, and Sir Gawain became the lead members of the Implementation Teams. Their task was to take guidance from the Change Management Office and the King and implement the change initiatives throughout the kingdom.

At the end of the day they all went out for mead and meat. As they reviewed the proceedings, they were amazed at how much they had learned about the entire kingdom, and about each other. They all had a new appreciation for each territory and how each territories actions impacted all of the others, sometimes not in positive ways. It was amazing to them and started to change their way of thinking. "This has been a hard, but very good day! We have to find a way to give our subjects the same experience."

Merlin smiled.

Communications Efforts

The Implementation Teams went straight to work developing the Communications plan. Armed with a well thought out Stakeholder analysis, they developed messages for each audience.

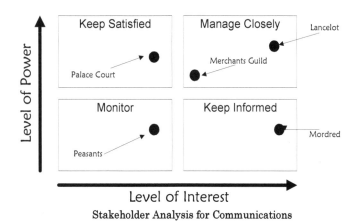

Stakeholder Analysis for Communications

The Implementation Teams commissioned placards with the Four Cornerstones to be made and hung in public places throughout the kingdom. The Palace Court received a monthly newsletter. The local town criers were commissioned to deliver a monthly message to everyone from merchants and craftsmen to farmers and peasants. To make the messages memorable, they used the following slogans:

- Round is Sound
- Got Chivalry?
- With a name like Camelot, it's got to be good!
- Equality. See more. Do more.

Most importantly, the entire effort was kicked off with a bang! The knights held simultaneous meetings in all of the territories with balloons, streamers, jousting, games and giveaways for the locals. The message of Equality, Chivalry and Justice was handed down and embraced by all.

And the knights of the Implementation Team smiled.

Territorial Involvement

While the king and Lancelot were making preparations for the construction and delivery of the round table, the Implementation Team was busy scheduling and holding Territorial Workshops. These workshops, similar to the Key Leader's Workshop they attended, would be used to design and document the new Business Model for the entire kingdom.

The workshops were held in all territories and included participants at all levels. The members of the Implementation Teams knew that including the people who actually perform the work was just as important (and maybe even more important) as including those who supervised it—as long as they were provided a forum where they feel free to speak and participate without retribution.

The Change Management Office proved to be excellent facilitators and the workshops went well. Everyone from nobility to peasants contributed. They began to see beyond their own little patches of land to the bigger picture of the kingdom, discovered how some of their practices did not contribute to the overall well-being of the kingdom. They devised new approaches, new processes, and new procedures to follow. Then they designed measures of success for each new initiative; a way to measure when the transformation was complete and a way to measure progress they were operating in a steady state.

It was an enormous amount of work and data to track. Merlin was apparently a very good magician, because he developed a highly integrated, relational database, as well as a method for gathering, tracking, and reporting data that he called "Pathfinder". Lancelot thought it was brilliant!

And Lancelot smiled.

Trouble in the Kingdom

With large, sweeping, change there are always resistors. For the most part, though, the process of going through the workshops and being able to see (often for the first time) their direct contribution to the kingdom was enough to bring everyone around. But, alas, the effort was not completely without incident.

While the transformation effort was beginning to take hold in all areas of the kingdom, there was a small, but growing area of discontent. In the southern territory of Wales, near the Camlan Valley, Mordred discovered there were some people opposed to the Transformation. He traveled to the area before the workshops were held with the sole intent to stir things up, spread rumors, and start a rebellion against the new Kingdom. (Maybe he could even overthrow Arthur and take the throne - and Gwennie - for himself.) His efforts were gaining speed and discontent with the effort was gaining speed.

Mordred had been trying to thwart the effort from the beginning, but this was the first time his efforts had become more than a nuisance that had to be dealt with. The Implementation Team was growing weary of cleaning up Mordred's mess, and this time it was more than a mess; it was a **threat** to the entire effort. This time drastic measures were called for.

The Implementation Team, Change Management Office, and Arthur all convened for a meeting. Topic # 1: *How to deal with Mordred.* After much discussion, they concluded that there was only one way to stop Mordred on his crusade to sabotage the transformation. No one liked the idea, Arthur least of all, but they had to remove Mordred from the Order of Knights. Quickly and quietly Mordred was stripped of his knighthood. He quickly lost what little power he once had. The Change Management Office sent Sir Kay to run the Wales workshops, thus ensuring that the people would have a true visionary to follow. And they not only followed Sir Kay, but they became the most productive region in the kingdom, and the biggest champions of the change. Seems, all they really wanted was for someone to listen to their concerns.

In the end all of the territories had a complete grasp of the new vision for the Kingdom, a clear picture of what their roles were and how they contributed to the prosperity and well being off all the other territories, and they had a roadmap to follow to institute the changes necessary for the Kingdom to fully realize the new vision.

And King Arthur smiled.

The Celebration

All the territories were working hard. From the roadmaps they developed the detailed implementation plans. The Change Management Office consolidated these plans into an Integrated Master Schedule. One by one the territories began meeting or beating their milestones for change. This success made people happy, and productivity was definitely on the rise. Merlin kept the dashboard updated and communications flowing. There was a great sense of accomplishment and pride among all subjects. Even Mordred, though no longer a knight, started to agree that this change was significant, and a good thing for the entire kingdom. The days of war and poverty were, at long last, over.

Soon came the day that the round table, the symbol of all four cornerstones of the transformation, was to be delivered. The Transformation Team declared that a great feast and celebration should be held on that day for every subject in the kingdom. The great feast was held in Camelot and all subjects from near and far were welcome to attend. For those who could not make the trip to the kingdom, additional festivities were planned in each of the Territories. And so that everyone, even servants and peasants, could participate the king hired the finest servants and chefs from France to cater all of the events. Thus, not only providing a special event for his subjects, but also promoting his newly transformed Kingdom outside of Briton, gaining international recognition, and maybe even leading to an award.

And the entire kingdom smiled.

And they lived happily … for a very long while.

THE END

Summary: Nuggets of Transformation Truth

I: Develop compelling and unambiguous transformation cornerstones.

- Cornerstones: 3-4 Clearly stated and aligned with overall vision and organizational strategy
- Cornerstone Objectives: 3-5 for each cornerstone, measurable, detailed, target the transformation
- The "So What" test: Does each objective lead to the cornerstone? Is it measurable? Is there a compelling reason to complete it?

II: Understand the best-practice methods for managing change

- Change Management is about behavior change
- Treat change management just like project management:
  - Define requirements
  - Design a blueprint and work plan
  - Plan and implement the design
  - Evaluate the work plan activities

III: Empower dedicated transformation management resources

- Dedicated Transformation Manager whose only job is to monitor and manage the change project
- Change Implementation Teams - Implement change within the ranks. Must implement the roadmap without interrupting service to their customers.

IV: Communicate relentlessly

- Create a sense of urgency: shining benefits of change, dire consequences of not changing
- Focus on stakeholders who have both power and influence
- Communicate roles, accountabilities and expectations

V: Design with the end in sight

"Keep your eyes on the prize." If you know where you are going, you have a much better chance of getting there.

- The Operations Blueprint
  - o Detailed job impact analysis to identify key operational outcomes
  - o Develop discrete job-level procedures for impacted operational outcomes
  - o Provide training, tools, and equipment to operate in new environment with the new capabilities that are required to enable the operational outcomes
  - o Define accountabilities across organizational/functional borders
  - o Create detailed process and job task definitions
- Don't cut corners on the Operations Blueprint
- Keep the sponsor out of the weeds

VI: Pick winnable battles and celebrate them

- Win early, win often, and always win
- Celebrate every win to demonstrate relentless progress
- Separate the easy from the hard
- Avoid public executions, but use them when necessary
- Converting a powerful resistor is the best possible victory

VII: Create and follow a transformation roadmap

- Centerpiece of the Transformation Plan
- High level look at the master plan of achievement
- Cornerstones, Objectives, and Operations Blueprint feed the Capability Development Roadmap
- The Roadmap feeds the Communication Strategy and the Integrated Master Schedule

VIII: Know the Resources required for transformation

- Transformation manager owns and manages the Master Schedule and resources
- Transformation Management ≠ Operations Management
- Building the capabilities to implement the operations blueprint
- Budget for Transformation
- Be flexible and set up a Change Control Board
- Establish accountability

Transformation Roles:

- o Sponsor
- o Transformation manager
- o Implementation teams
- o Employees

IX: Employ a system to manage the volumes of data and complexity

Develop an information management strategy for the transformation

- Enterprise Architecture management system
- Document management / knowledge management system
- Learning management system
- Project management system

X: Measure and communicate progress, risk, and accountability

- Develop a highly visible transformation dashboard
- Measure progress toward transformation milestones
- Enforce accountability for change
- Risk and issue management
- Executive transformation management
- Communicate progress, risks, issues, and accountabilities to all stakeholders
- Visibility promotes healthy competition
- Transformation manager manages the transformation dashboard

Authors' Acknowledgements

We'd like to take the opportunity to recognize those individuals who inspired us, educated us, and helped make this book possible. One of these great businessmen is Charles Harris—perhaps the smartest executive we've ever had the pleasure of working with. Thanks Charlie, for letting us tap your vast experience and prodigious intellect, and thanks for the lovely foreword.

Our most shining executive role models were Stan Walz and Barry "Boo" Harner of VectorCSP, from whom we learned the value of strong, consistent leadership and the importance of integrity and honor. The program management team at VectorCSP also played a key role in developing the transformation architecture conveyed by this book. We'd especially like to acknowledge the contributions of Robert Burnett, Dr. Nicola McMullan, Damien Walz, Frank Holman, Ray Reid, Bill Kopp, Stan Nielsen, and Roger Knowles along with all the other members of the Vector team who labored to make enterprise transformation a success for large government agencies.

Next we'd like to recognize the change management gurus on whose mighty shoulders we humbly stand. This book would not have been possible without their contributions to the state-of-the art in change management. Those of you who are students of change management will recognize these names, including John Kotter, Dan S. Cohen, John Kay, Warren Bennis, Charles Handy, John Hayes, Chip and Dan Heath, and many others. Go read their books. Seriously.

We'd also like to recognize the indomitable Ron Simms of the Mason School of Business at the College of William and Mary for his encouragement and voluminous classroom presentations that guided us through many perils. Thanks, Professor Simms.

Finally, we'd like to apologize for the liberties taken in re-imagining the Arthurian legend for our purposes. If you'd like to read the original legend, check out the medieval stories of Le Morte d'Arthur by Thomas Mallory or a modern retelling like The Once and Future King by T.S. White (or just for fun go watch Monty Python's Quest for the Holy Grail).

Patrick Cumby
Rosalind Lambeth
Alexandria, VA
March 2012

Made in the USA
Charleston, SC
19 July 2012